SHAR

JOURNEY

Lessons from my students and clients with tangled tongues

To: Melissa,
with Admiration & Affection

Lon L. Emerick

Lon Emerick

Illustrations by Diana Magnuson

ISBN 0-96-50577-6-3

Library of Congress Card Number 00-106637

Published by North Country Publishing
355 Heidtman Road
Skandia, Michigan 49885
906-942-7879

Printed in the United States of America

First Edition 2001

10 9 8 7 6 5 4 3 2 1

For First Daughters Lynn Elizabeth and Mary Ellen

"... if I repent of anything, it is very likely to be my good behavior.
What demon possessed me that I behaved so well?"

Henry David Thoreau

PREFACE

In the beginning there was communication: The transmission of messages connects all living things in an endless ebb and flow of information. Brontosauruses did it; birds do it; even honey bees do it. There is even evidence that trees and plants send out chemical messages summoning suitable predators when other insects attack their foliage. But it is in human beings that we witness a remarkably facile means of exchanging information—the use of language.

Language is the glue that binds humans together. Words are like magic wands that lend some order and predictability in a constantly shifting environment. The ability to speak, to use spoken language, is the pinnacle of human achievement and as such is *the* vital prerequisite for human interaction. It is silence which isolates.

The act of speaking, sharing one's mind through the vehicle of words, is so natural and so integral to being human that when a person is unable to talk normally, the impact is pervasive. It invades all aspects of the person's life. A speech disability can and often does have devastating consequences.

What if you could not share your mind by way of your mouth? How would you acquire the good things in life—the joy of friendship, the satisfaction of earning a living, the winning of a mate, the pride of self-respect? Only those who are denied the magic of spoken words can appreciate the awesome power of this instrument that humans have invented.

Our society does not suffer the speech-disabled gladly and those so afflicted know a special kind of misery. I have negotiated the peaks and valleys of speech pathology for many years—first as a client and then as a therapist—and know its frustrations and challenges very well. Having been born again at the age of 21 when I first managed to achieve some freedom from stuttering, I opted to devote a professional lifetime helping others grasp the miracle of spoken words.

For more than 30 years I labored in the groves of academe, at Moorhead State University and Northern Arizona University, but longest and most happily at Northern Michigan University. I was privileged to assist scores of students become speech and hearing clinicians. Since I always seem to attract a family wherever I happen to be, students adopted me, first as a big brother, then a father-figure and then—time to retire!—a grandfather.

Most individuals entering the field of speech therapy are female and I have over the years acquired quite a retinue of surrogate daughters. They shared so much of themselves and enriched my life in a myriad of ways. Working closely together with our clients, we weathered the crises, celebrated the triumphs and shared the indescribable joy of serving others with enthusiasm and good humor.

An explanation about some of the humorous incidents the reader will find in this book is now in order. Let me say at the outset that I have a zany sense of humor—less kind observers maintain that I am congenitally silly—and if laughter is nature's best tonic, then I must have a corner on prescriptions. But it was during my early years in college, when I worked as an orderly on the midnight shift in an urban hospital emergency room, that I discovered how jocularity and dark comedy are used to relieve tension and anguish. At first I was astonished at the way nurses and physicians turned to humor to lessen the impact of catastrophic injuries confronting them each night. Although I had used comical banter all my life to defuse negative responses to my stuttering, I didn't realize that many persons in the helping professions employ M*A*S*H* humor as a cleansing tool for psychic relief. We mean no disrespect for the disabled nor is it our intent to hold them up to ridicule. If we did not have the safety valve of humor, as inappropriate as it may sometimes appear to people in other lines of work, we would be weeping. An example from my experience in the speech clinic may clarify what I am trying to say:

> Amy Beckett, a three-year-old child, was brought to the speech clinic with the complaint that she was beginning to stutter. During the interview with Mrs. Beckett, she revealed that there was considerable pressure in the home for all family members to follow her husband's somewhat unreasonable standard of order and cleanliness. All of the family shoes had to be lined up with military precision, the door knobs were to be washed after every use and the house vacuumed daily.
>
> James Beckett owned and operated a very successful local service station. Mrs. Beckett reported that her husband put a sign on the wall of the station reading, "Let us all be emissaries of neatness." Clearly this excessive need for order and perfection was having a negative impact on Amy's developing speech skills.
>
> In addition to other recommendations, I suggested that Mrs. Beckett show Amy in some small way—such as leaving a wet towel lying on the bathroom floor after taking a shower—that no one has to be perfect.
>
> The morning after my counseling session with Mrs. Beckett, I heard an angry male voice in the reception area of the clinic.
>
> "Where will I find that s.o.b.?" the voice demanded loudly.
>
> "Down at the end of the hall in office number 10," responded the secretary without a pause.
>
> Shortly thereafter, a man who had to be Mr. Beckett appeared at the doorway of my office holding a damp towel. "Are you the s.o.b. who is breaking up my happy home?" he bellowed, brandishing the towel. "My wife said you told her to leave this towel lying in the bathroom!"
>
> A sarcastic retort came quickly to mind—"What makes you think you have a happy home?"—and an involuntary surge of anger tightened my

chest. But I knew I must defuse Mr. Beckett's hostility quickly. Remembering the principle of semantic satiation (that words lose meaning with repeated utterance), I proceeded to use the angry epithet over and over again.

"I am the s.o.b. who has been talking with your wife about Amy's fluency problem," I said. "Would you please sit down. The s.o.b. has to make a phone call, and then the s.o.b. will be free to chat with you."

Picking up the phone, I dialed my wife (who has endured all manner of curious encounters because of her husband's profession), and said, "This is the s.o.b. calling. I was wondering what we were having for dinner. Okay. The s.o.b. will be home early."

Turning to Mr. Beckett, I announced, "Now, the s.o.b. is through and ready for a chat."

By that time, Mr. Beckett was chuckling softly. I wish I could say that this one incident led to perfect communication between the therapist and the parent. Although I had managed to disarm Amy's father with humor, I knew that obsessive-compulsive behavior is very difficult to alter. Deep anxieties are bound up in the rituals of cleanliness and orderliness. I was not surprised when, at the father's insistence, the Beckett family withdrew from treatment.

Therapists share the despair, frustration, even the anger of scores of children and adults. In order to be effective, we must keep healthy the instrument of cure—the therapist. You can't heal a wound with a dirty bandage and all humans are soiled by the business of living from time to time. Laughter is one of the best antidotes to the toxicity of misery.

Lon L. Emerick

West Branch Township

The Superior Peninsula

July 12, 2000

CONTENTS

Prologue 1

Foster Creek Dreaming 7

Life Is a Journey 12

Don't Pole Vault Over Mouse Turds 20

Prize Those Times When You Are Thwarted or Frustrated 31

Don't Wear a Raincoat in The Shower 40

The Law of The Echo 50

There You Are 59

Let the Craziness Emerge 76

Restoring Balance 84

Facts and Attitude 93

Keep Looking for the Pony 102

Epilogue 112

Prologue

None of my university course work prepared me for this clinical encounter, I thought ruefully as I scanned the notes I had outlined so carefully before the session. Here I was, a new assistant professor, freshly anointed with a Ph.D. degree, the author of a widely-acclaimed pamphlet on interviewing parents and I was stymied by the taciturn Mr. Taminen. He dismissed my persistent inquiries about treatment options for his nonverbal teenager with dogmatic finality. "Most people, day talk too much anyway, eh," he pronounced and thumped a calloused hand on the table for emphasis. The vibrations pulsated through the wood and exaggerated the trembling of my own fingers.

The director of the speech clinic, several colleagues and a group of advanced students were observing my diagnostic session through a two-way mirror and I could sense their restlessness as they shifted impatiently on creaky metal chairs in the adjacent room. The prickly damp warmth of anxiety began to creep up my neck and, although I wasn't about to abandon my efforts to reach the client, I could detect the far off and muted bleat of panic. I must stop thinking about myself, I thought, and focus on the parent. Abandoning my own discomfort, I leaned forward and scrutinized Mr. Taminen closely while plotting my next move.

A stout man in his late 60s, Eurpo Taminen shifts uneasily in his chair. Clearly he is out of his element in the speech clinic and very ill at ease. His face, deeply furrowed from years of exposure to the harsh northern climate on his hardscrabble farm, is ruddy and a stubble of salt and pepper whiskers gives him a grizzled look. Wisps of iron gray hair peek out from under a greasy baseball cap proclaiming *Purina Feeds*. He is clad in a faded plaid shirt and tattered overalls. The small examining room was uncomfortably warm when we entered and now the unmistakable aroma of pig manure caking Mr. Taminen's boots emanates upward in heavy, odoriferous waves.

"Yep," he uttered softly in a peculiar inhaled vocalization I had never heard before. He repeated the inhaled "Yep" two more times and then, as if for emphasis, he added, "Yah, sure, you betcha." He thumped the table again.

Later I would learn that many old time residents of Michigan's Upper Peninsula, particularly those of Finnish descent, do not always communicate with strangers in a linear fashion. They talk obliquely. My ignorance of correct communicative protocol cost me the opportunity to acquire a nice piece of hunting property. I simply approached the owner one day and asked him how much he wanted for the 40-acre tract. His abrupt withdrawal and subsequent reticence astonished me. When I expressed my bewilderment to a real estate broker, himself a second-generation Finn, he laughed tightly and changed the topic. When I pressed him, he offered an explanation.

"You never just come right out and ask, 'What do you want for that land?' You gotta, well, sorta sidle up to the topic. Take it slow. Talk about the weather, the blueberry crop, whatever. Then, gradually—it helps to be a little indifferent—you might say, 'If a fella were ever to sell some land, say, like this here 40, what do you think it might be worth?' "

Not only *what* one says, but *how* one says it, I also learned, can be peculiar to the Upper Peninsula. Heard more often in certain rural areas, the regional accent is characterized by vocal and phonetic features: a lilting melody pattern, substitution of *d* and *t* sounds for *th*, and adding an "aye" or "eh" at the end of declarative sentences. New residents, as I once was, not only have some trouble decoding Yoopers (as they proudly call themselves) but the minute we open our mouths, we are marked as newcomers. And newcomers are notorious not only for poking fun at natives of the Peninsula, but also have an annoying tendency to think they must bring "modern culture" to this remote region.

Maybe that was one reason why Mr. Taminen was so resistant to my efforts to determine the history of his son's language problem. Even though most residents in the remote area of the family farm knew about the retarded son who had never gone to school, they respected the parents' wishes to keep the boy at home. Then Congress passed the Education for All Handicapped Children Act. Under this legislation, all disabled children between the ages of three and twenty-one years of age must be identified, a careful assessment made of their needs, and a comprehensive plan or an individualized educational program developed. Armed with the new statute, a new and very zealous consultant in special education for the school district went to Mr. Taminen and delivered an ultimatum: His son, Toysto, must be evaluated at the university speech and hearing clinic to determine the best placement and treatment. Reluctantly, and only because of the implied threat to take away his son, the elderly farmer came to the clinic. Now he sat across from me, arms crossed over his huge chest, solid, enduring. "Yep," he sighed again in that strange inhaled voice.

Suddenly, I remembered something my grandfather told me about Finnish people years ago: *SISU*. As a young man of 16, my maternal grandfather emigrated from his native Cornwall, England to work in the booming copper mines of Northern Michigan. It was a harsh life in a hard, flinty land and only the strong of mind and body survived. A trait my grandfather came to admire in Finnish Americans working beside him in the mines—and grandfather did not suffer the weak gladly—was what they termed *SISU*. Roughly defined, it is the ability to confront adversity with courage, endurance and tenacity. One takes care of one's own and does not complain.

Hesitantly, I observed, "Mr. Taminen, you have coped for some time now with the trouble your son has . . . "

"What trouble?" he interrupted, "Toysto, he's not quite right in da head, but he don't need no help from nobody. He can stay on da farm wit' me like always."

Slowly, the story unfolded. Toysto, now age 15, is the youngest of five children. He surprised his parents by coming along when Mr. Taminen was 54 and his wife, Helmi, was 49. Right from the beginning they knew something was wrong with the child. He was slow to crawl, slow to walk and he never did learn to talk. The Taminens were embarrassed about their disabled youngster and wanted to spare him the pain of dealing with other children and the demands of school. So they kept Toysto at home, often hiding him in the basement or barn when strangers appeared at the farm. Mrs. Taminen died two years ago and all the other children have grown up and moved away.

"It's Toysto and me," said Mr. Taminen, "and he's a good boy, eh. Real strong he is. He helps me cultivate and you should see him dig potatoes."

The Taminen's 40-acre subsistence farm is located in a very remote area west of Marquette. Mr. Taminen and his son live on the father's small military pension and the sale of potatoes, their only cash crop. An ancient dairy cow supplies milk, a pig is butchered every year. They get by. It was doubtful that Mr. Taminen could make it without the help of his son. But what would happen to Toysto when the father dies? What can we do to fulfill the needs of this youngster?

The first thing one notices about Toysto are his powerful forearms and massive hands. He carries his arms close to his torso, elbows bent, with the huge hands protruding outward at chest level. Slowly he rotates his thumbs and forefingers in a clockwise direction, opening and closing in a pincer-like movement. With each hand closure, he utters, "I-uh," as if he has something important to share but has lost his train of thought. Although Toysto seemed to hear normally and could follow simple directions, he had no expressive language. During the examination the youngster refused to sit still and paced around the room rotating his enormous hands and softly crooning, "I-uh." The prognosis for improvement did not look favorable; children who do not develop language by five or six years of age are not likely ever to acquire much facility with the spoken word.

Following the assessment, the diagnostic team debated where to settle Toysto while I finished the interview with Mr. Taminen. At that time our clinic was small and, with other therapy going on, space was limited. Remembering that his father reported that Toysto liked quiet, dark places, the team ushered him into a small room used to house client files and store office materials, reassured him that his father would return shortly and turned out the lights. Toysto paced slowly about the perimeter of the room, rotating his powerful hands and softly chanting the enigmatic "I-uh." He seemed as contented as he could be in a strange environment. We thought he would not be disturbed. We didn't count on Mandy.

Mandy Hildreth was one of the very few students I have known who made me wince when I just thought about her. An older woman who returned to school after raising her children, she treated the faculty and fellow students as errant youngsters who needed a strong mother figure. She was officious and peremptory as she went about her self-appointed role. A short, plump woman with very prominent breasts, she patrolled the clinic looking for infractions: the soap in the ladies' restroom needed replacing; the corners of the audiological testing booth were dusty; there was a scrap of paper on the floor in the waiting room. Nothing escaped her attention. Mandy carried herself in a stiff, upright posture which exaggerated her generous endowments. She was continually barging into my office to register a complaint. Her fellow students just smiled tightly, rolled their eyes and stayed out of her way. But now Mandy was headed for a memorable collision with Toysto.

Mandy noticed the closed and darkened file room immediately; usually it was open and well lit. In her impetuous style, she charged in to remedy the infraction just as Toysto was approaching the door on his circuit of the room. Severely startled by her abrupt appearance, he grasped the most prominent part of her anatomy in his strong hands. Equally astonished, Mandy let out a Wagnerian bellow and began hitting out at and kicking Toysto. The frightened lad tightened his grip and, locked together, Toysto and Mandy did a wild dance of pain and fright around the small room.

The entire staff of the speech and hearing clinic rushed to the sound of Mandy's screams and tried to disentangle the frantic dancers. But it was Mr. Taminen who rescued Mandy; he talked soothingly to Toysto and slowly the frightened boy relinquished his grip. Then Mr. Taminen did something totally unexpected: he began to chuckle. Slow and quiet at first, it soon evolved into raucous belly-laughing and he collapsed on the floor in uncontrolled mirth. Laughter like that is contagious and soon we all joined Mr. Taminen in the tension-relieving merriment. All except Mandy, who adjusted her clothes and stalked off in high dudgeon.

It would make a nice story if this one incident led to a clinical breakthrough and, after several weeks of speech therapy, Toysto started speaking in compound sentences. But that only happens in the movies. During the lengthy administrative process of determining the proper educational site for his son, Mr. Taminen died of congestive heart failure. None of his older siblings could or would care for Toysto so he was placed in a residential facility for disabled persons. A trial program of therapy yielded no positive results; it was more annoying than helpful for the teenager. However, despite his lack of spoken language, Toysto adjusted well to the group home. The last time I saw him, several years ago, he smiled enigmatically when I entered the room. Perhaps, he, too, remembers the Dance of the Wild Cucumber with Mandy in the file room.

FOSTER CREEK DREAMING

Time is running out—I can't delay the task any longer. The memo from the university records office highlights the terse message in strident yellow: *All grades are due by 4 p.m. on May 2nd.* With some distaste, I open the large brown envelope and spill out the rosters of the classes I taught during the winter semester. It is time for the semiannual alphabet game.

"Oh, how I detest this part of teaching," I mutter. I loathe giving tests, scoring them and watching some students' faces when they get the unhappy news. The entire concept of grading is based on a silly premise: That after 16 weeks of reading, writing, talking, listening and thinking (even after all these years I am still an optimist), I can pop out of a box and pronounce "C" or "B+." How can that simple letter describe what went on? Surely it would take at least a paragraph to summarize adequately what had transpired from January to late April.

Alas, however, grading is embedded deep in the soul of the academy. Students expect it, parents demand it, even educated deans foster it. Yeah, right. Well, enough already with the negative musing, professor. Time to get to work.

So now I will add up all the scores on quizzes, tests, assigned papers and compute an overall score: 90 to 100 is an A, 80 to 89, a B; in short I attempt to quantify each student's performance. I must remember not to transpose columns in the grade book—such tedious work with the sun shining so gloriously outside.

I inspect the class roster sheets. Okay, here's the printout for Introduction to Speech Pathology; 87 students in that one (heavy sigh).

Then, Stuttering; only 18 upperclassmen in that offering. And, finally, Seminar in Voice Disorders, an enrollment of 11 graduate students; that will be the easiest.

Wait! What the hell is this other sheet? Phonetics and Speech Science. Enrollment 27 students. How . . . what happened? I don't remember—oh, my God! Here's a class assigned to me and I didn't meet it for the entire semester! Panic grips me as I tear through my grade book to find some reference to this ghost class. Are the students still languishing in the assigned room, cobwebs clinging to their idle pencils? My tendency to catastrophize kicks in and my thoughts race ahead to a somber summons from the Dean's office. A plaintive wail escapes my lips.

Then through the panic I hear my wife Lynn's soothing voice. "It's okay, it's okay, it's just a bad dream." I awaken and realize I'm in bed, sweating profusely and clutching the quilt in both hands. The fearful images drift away slowly and I smile ruefully about the tenacity of the familiar nighttime specters. The occupational hazard still lingers in my synapses after 10 years of retirement: It's the university instructor's nightmare again.

When I first started teaching at Northern Michigan University, I somewhat hesitantly shared this recurring nightmare with Jim Rapport, chairman of the department and my empathic mentor. Expecting some insightful and calming counsel, I was surprised when Jim laughed uncontrollably. "It goes with the territory," he gasped when he finally gained control "We all experience some variation of the same bad dream."

Weak-kneed with relief, I got out of bed to relish the tranquility of the morning to which I had awakened. Padding into the living room of our log home, I paused, as I always do, and gazed out at the forest. Situated on the very edge of a heavily forested ravine, the room is dominated by a bank of large windows which seem to bring the trees right into the house. Living here is like a wonderful dream, I mused, the perfect antidote to those nightmare-inducing remnants of my professional life.

With a mug of coffee, I returned to my favorite chair to watch the unfolding of a gorgeous spring day. And what a magnificent morning it was! As I admired the dew sparkling on the soft greens of May in the slanting sunlight, I celebrated the triumph of pleasant daydreams over nightmares and the return of spring to the north.

It is difficult for people who live in warmer climes to understand why spring is such a major—indeed magical—event in the north. The joy of open water, a bare sun-warmed hillside, or the first wildflower cannot truly be appreciated simply by coming north for the spring. Only after you have lived through an extended winter, endured the many storms, the short twilight days, and the weeks of frigid arctic air, can you begin to understand our longing for some harbinger of warmth. It becomes terribly important to find evidence of new life: snowmelt around the trunk of a birch tree; a clump of willows wearing a new tiara of soft gray buds; the faint scent of trailing arbutus. For those of us addicted to the many charms of spring, these early transformations are an annual epiphany.

Nature has always provided the tonic I need; now as I sat admiring the valley and the ridges beyond, the restiveness of my rude awakening was gone and I reveled in the many shades of green. Unlike the bold splashes of color which announce the arrival of fall, the spring display is understated, subdued and very delicate. The new leaves unfold in pastel hues. It looks as if an artist dipped a giant brush in several shades of green and touched the hillsides softly, hesitantly. The spruce and pine in their dark coats punctuate and highlight the harmonious mixture of soft green. Later this morning I will drive toward town and witness the greening of the north against the immense blueness of Lake Superior.

Before I yield to the invitation of a spring morning, perhaps it is good to pause and reflect on the journey that led me here to this place at this time. Life, I have found, is a wondrous adventure, an unfolding pilgrimage to be *lived*, not a problem to be solved. Along the way, I have been fortunate enough to discover bits of wisdom, some guidelines that helped me negotiate the peaks and valleys of my personal odyssey. I formulated the guidelines into ten fundamental principles—maxims—of how to conduct a wise and happy life.

Where did these ten maxims come from? I wish I could be sure, but I think they were gleaned from several sources: life with a slow and halting tongue, many speech disabled persons with whom I have worked, a myriad of students who enriched my life on a daily basis, several mentors, both literary and personal, friends who shared the trail and lightened my load, and a healthy appreciation for serendipity.

I have tried to keep the maxims—my touchstones—as simple as possible and to illustrate them with memorable events from fifty years in the velvet embrace of speech therapy. Some words of caution may be in order:

Be flexible in the application of any maxim. Be wary of anyone—most of all yourself—who has rigid assumptions about the way the world works. Watch out for "hardening of the categories," that dread disease of thinking whereby a mental groove becomes so wide and deep you can't climb out of it.

One time I examined an adult who had suffered a severe stroke and was afflicted with a severe case of aphasia, a disorder which renders individuals virtually incapable of using language. Heino Maki had global aphasia: he could neither receive nor express information. To all of my questions, including all the tasks on a standard measure of aphasia, he replied, "Heino" (sounds like "I know"). We all assumed that his prognosis was very poor, and arranged for custodial care. But before we made final arrangements, I asked a graduate student to give Mr. Maki another test of aphasia, mostly to provide her with some experience in diagnostic methods. Karlyn did not know of our findings and approached Mr. Maki with a fresh perspective. When Heino simply continued to utter "Heino" in response to every question, she thought he was saying, "I know, I know" and she said to him firmly, "I know you know, Mr. Maki, now say the word." Damned if he didn't start naming the objects she presented to him!

Don't sail under false colors. A story about a former client and his student therapist will, I think, make this admonition clear:

> Mike, a severe stutterer from Indiana, came to our clinic for a three-week intensive therapy program. As head of his therapy team, I assigned a male student, Tim, to coordinate and perform most of the treatment. Both outdoorsmen, Tim and Mike established instant rapport. However, Mike, a thoughtful well-read accountant, was amused by Tim's attempt to demonstrate his new and only partly acquired vocabulary. Tim was addicted to malapropisms: he would report that some relative of his had major surgery and was under the "antiseptic" for six hours, that he watched the smoke "bellering" out of the cabin chimney in the cold weather, or that some university administrator had made him so angry it got his "dandruff" up.
>
> Finally, one day beside the Escanaba River while the three of us were grouse hunting, Mike skewered Tim with a pithy comment. Tim had just reported that a forest road he was following in search of game had "dissipated." Looking Tim right in the eye and with a smile on his face, Mike observed, "Tim, you're trying to shit higher than your ass."

Make the maxims active. The ten maxims are guidelines for behavior, not abstractions. Test, revise and make them your own touchstones for the journey of life. In one of his letters, Keats put it this way:

> Axioms in philosophy are not axioms until they are proved upon our pulses: We read fine things but never feel them to the full until we have gone the same steps as the author.

After years of searching, I have found the goal of my own pilgrimage here at our Foster Creek Homestead. Surrounded by densely forested ridges and valleys and an extensive wetland along Foster Creek, our home is in a country paradise. Dwelling here in harmony with the natural world, I know what it means to live well.

LIFE IS A JOURNEY

Life is filled with fear and frustration when you speak with a slow and halting tongue. Even my fantasies about living well were dismal until, at the age of 21, I was born again, not in the evangelical sense, but in being released from the bondage of stuttering.

Stuttering is an astonishing and absurd act, which confuses, amuses and sometimes exasperates listeners. Talking is so easy, so automatic for most people. "Why don't you simply go ahead and say your name," friends asked me, "instead of stopping and starting and jerking around like that?" That's easy for *them* to say! Only those who have speech defects know how crucial oral communication is and how devastating the consequences when it is impaired. Broken speech, I learned quite early, is painful for both speaker and listener.

The origins of my stuttering are buried somewhere in the interstices of old family memories and sibling relationships. I probably started when I was quite young. There is some hint that my speech was marred by abnormal repetitions and hesitations even before I started kindergarten at four years old. My parents did not like to discuss the topic. Later, when I pressed my father for details of my early speech acquisition, he demurred cryptically, "You don't talk about rope in a house where a man has been hanged."

The first time I remember having any real difficulty talking occurred in the first grade. My family had moved during the summer, so I was the new kid in the neighborhood and in my grade at school. I was a bit apprehensive about beginning with a new teacher and new classmates, but I was also excited about learning to read. On the first day of class, the teacher asked each student in turn to give his or her name. When she came to me, suddenly I was totally blocked, unable to utter even a squeak. Even now, six decades later, I remember the shock and terror which engulfed me. Transfixed with panic, I sat there mutely, a zombie, the living dead! Finally, (it took less than 15 seconds but seemed an eternity) a friendly girl who lived next door to my new home introduced me to the class.

It was all downhill after that terrifying episode in the first grade. School, with its many demands for verbal responses, was particularly difficult and I must have been a burden to my teachers. They offered me the usual timeworn helps that don't really help, like "Stop and start over again," "Take a deep breath," and "Think what you are going to say." They said words for me when my verbal parturition became too painful to see and hear. One fourth grade teacher, however, found what she considered an excellent use for my hesitant speech. Whenever she discovered her lesson plans running short, she would call upon me to read. I was sure to use up the remaining time. My days were filled with intense surges of anxiety and humiliation.

Most people can sympathize with the embarrassment of stuttering, but they don't realize the inner frustration that results when you have to order lemon or strawberry sodas because your favorite, chocolate, is too difficult to say; walking down many flights of stairs because you are unable to say, "First floor, please" to the elevator attendant. In restaurants, the words, "I'll have the same," or "Same here" spared me the ordeal of ordering for myself, but often brought me foods I disliked. My response to all this embarrassment and frustration, strange as it may seem, took two forms: to clobber my adversaries or play the role of clown.

Woe be unto anyone who teased, smiled or even blinked when I stuttered. I literally fought my way through junior and senior high schools; in college, fortunately, my hair-trigger temper was channeled into the boxing ring by a wise dormitory advisor. I got a measure of respect, if not acceptance, from my male peers; I couldn't talk but my fists could. In some social situations, I was tolerated if I fulfilled the role of mascot but never became a real member of the group. I'm sure that none of my high school chums would have wanted me to date, let alone marry, their sisters.

Humor was my other foil. In circumstances where I couldn't punch someone out, I turned to jokes to reduce tension and distract my listeners. Amazingly, when I joked around, I stuttered only mildly and at times I was totally fluent. But I had to originate the humor—persons who stutter are outraged that their speech disorder is still used by comedians to elicit laughs. I used comedy so much in high school that I was designated as a class clown. Discovering that I was a better-than-average mimic, I made shambles of recitation periods by imitating celebrities or even the teacher. My old high school buddies still speak reverently of one pun I pulled off in chemistry class. The teacher gave brief weekly exams which, for some reason, he termed "quizzies." They were very difficult. As the instructor passed back the fourth such quiz, and I saw that I had again failed it, I remarked *Soto voce*, "If this is a quizzie, I sure would hate to see one of his testies."

But it was all a charade and underneath my jester's costume I was desperate for relief from my stuttering nemesis.

My parents, too, were desperate. I could tell by the furtive worried glances they exchanged and their heavy, long-suffering sighs that my hesitant speech bothered them deeply. Even as a young child, I found it strange and disconcerting that they never talked to me directly about my stuttering problem. The topic was taboo in our family and I felt terribly isolated and unclean; stuttering must be a nasty, unmentionable problem, I thought.

My three brothers, all normal speakers, seemed to get far more "atta boys" (my father's form of praise) than I did. It hurt also to be the family pariah, the abnormal son who required special handling and expensive treatments. My parents tried to get help for me but unfortunately therapy for stuttering, or any type of speech disorder, was very limited in the 1930s and 40s.

There was very little effective public school therapy in those early days and so I explored all the old home remedies. I sang words, I practiced breath control, I tried to relax. One summer, I even ruined my teeth talking with pebbles in my mouth. None of these methods worked for long. After the initial distraction had worn off, I would be stuttering as badly as ever. Then my parents started searching for a magical cure.

In the not too distant past, stutterers were often preyed upon by charlatans. It was so easy to set up a "school of stammering," claim to have a secret cure, and promise total fluency with a few easy lessons. Differing techniques were used, but they boil down to the fact that by using some distracting device, a stutterer can gain temporary speech fluency. Such fluency usually lasted just long enough for the fee to be collected and the stutterer to be ushered out the door. Let me describe only one quack treatment program—the last one my parents tried.

The advertisement brochure was colorful, enticing, extravagant; it promised a total cure. Testimonials were included to buttress the claims of complete success. A photograph of the director and founder of the treatment center, looking very successful standing beside his Rolls Royce, was appended to the application form. How were my unsophisticated parents to know that the promises were hollow? So off I went for the two-week cure at a now-extinct Midwestern "School for Stammering."

For the first day or two the dozen adolescent boys in my "class" were admonished to observe strict silence. No talking was allowed. Then we were shown how to chant in unison as we lifted small dumbbells. Finally, near the end of the first week, the director introduced THE METHOD for curing stuttering. We were instructed never to reveal the secret formula, but now I believe it is safe to tell you about it. It was very simple: We were told to hold our right hands in front of our faces and time the utterance of each word with a firm pinch of our forefingers and thumb. The director and his assistants circulated among us, insisting that we say a word only at the precise moment of the pinch. If we stuttered, they told us that we did not time the word-pinch union correctly. If we were fluent, the pinching was declared perfect. We were informed that we now had the technique to cure our stuttering. If we followed it precisely, the director insisted, we would not stutter. He guaranteed it.

We practiced the technique in the dining room, we practiced it during recreation, we even practiced in the shower. A bolder member of our group finally voiced the reservation which all of us harbored about the finger-pinching routine.

"It's as bad as my old stuttering," he objected. "How the hell can I do this pinching stuff in public? People will think I'm nuts!"

The director smiled and smoothly suggested that after we learned the technique very well, we could simply put our hand in our pocket and pinch unnoticed. For the love of Heaven! Can you imagine how obscene it would look for teenage boys to repeatedly pinch their fingers in their pants pockets? And what were we to do when we went swimming? Not a one of us kept the secret pinching cure, not even as far as the railroad depot.

While I rode woefully toward home on the train after that latest futile attempt at solving the riddle of my stuttering, a kindly old gray-haired conductor stopped at my seat and asked my destination. I opened my mouth for the well-rehearsed "Detroit" but all that emerged was a series of muted gurgles. Finally, the old man peered at me over his glasses, shook his head and, with just a trace of a smile, said, "Well, young man, either express yourself or go by freight."

The conductor had shuffled on down the aisle of the rocking passenger car before the shock waves swept over me. Looking out the window at the speeding landscape through a tearful mist of anger and frustration, I felt the surreptitious glances of passengers seated nearby; a flush of crimson embarrassment crept slowly up my neck and my head throbbed with despair. Long afterwards I remembered the conductor's pointed comment. For years I licked that and other stuttering wounds and nursed my wrath to keep it warm, dreaming that someday I would right all those unrightable wrongs. But in the end his pithy pun changed my life. The old man, incredibly, had been right. Why indeed go by freight? Why let my journey through life be dictated by the timetable of stuttering? Alas, though, I am slow to learn and I went by freight, lugging a heavy load of stuttering, until my junior year in college.

Maxim 1. ***Life is a journey, not a destination***

Although we may have good friends and lovers on the trip, we travel down life's highway basically with ourselves, and we had better make sure we have a good companion. By focusing on being the best possible person we can be, there will be little time left for the futile task of trying to change or manage others. Let me offer one caveat: You will not "find yourself" by an obsessive inward pursuit. Paradoxically, when you pursue something else–seek something meaningful to learn or do–the self emerges from discipline and routine. "Lose yourself and maybe find yourself" is the refrain of the John Denver song.

Let me confess it right away: I'm still a pilgrim finding my way among the peaks and valleys. Still, showing more temerity than good sense, I cannot resist offering these guidelines which are beacons in my own quest:

- treat yourself and everyone (and everything) with respect
- seek simplicity, for it is complications which weigh us down and make the journey arduous
- practice joy, the simple delight of being alive on this wondrous planet
- strive for integrity: keep your word and be steadfast in your moral/ethical convictions
- honor the creative energy of life

What would I have done without Alma Nature during those early childhood years? Frustrated and bewildered by my speech problem, I turned to the soothing solace of the natural world. Fortuitously, my family lived then in a rural area. We had a milk cow, chickens and a huge garden. It was here that I first became aware of birds and kindled a passion that still burns brightly today, more than fifty years later.

During this era, I also bonded deeply with the northern wilds, an experience which was to have profound impact on where I wanted to live and work. I don't know why my over-protective mother let me spend several summers during WW II with my maternal grandparents on their 40-acre hobby farm. Their log cabin was located in a remote area near Oscoda in the northern Lower Peninsula and the environs were a bonanza for a small boy enamored with forests and streams. Each day we explored, picked wild berries, fished in Van Etten creek and let the joy of long quiet summer days wash over us like a soothing tide.

There is an abundant source of nurture in nature. I drank deeply of the tonic and by the time I reached adulthood and more fluent speech, the habit had indelibly marked my life. Nature is the most skillful therapist of all.

DON'T POLE VAULT OVER MOUSE TURDS

I stood tensely in the faded brown ranks of the university R.O.T.C. class. The sergeant squinted as he held the yellow class list at arm's length and called the roll. He had reached the Bs: "Bowman . . . Brooks." I would have to say, "Here, sir," when my name was called. Despite the chill of the late fall day, a trickle of perspiration slowly descended from my forehead and rolled down my nose. Just say "Here, sir . . . Here, sir," I repeated to myself.

"Cameron . . . Coleman," snapped the sergeant. Maybe if I licked my lips and then said, "HERE, sir."

The blood began to race through my head. I was sure my heart would burst. Then my name was called: "Emerick . . . Emerick!"

I opened my mouth for the well-rehearsed "Here, sir." Nothing would come. I pulled my abdominal muscles in hard to break the block in my throat . . . silence. I stole a glance at the sergeant who, by this time, had made a notation of my absence. I wanted to wave and shout, "Hey, it's me in here . . . I'm here!" I looked at the men in the ranks beside me. I felt a flush of embarrassment creep slowly up my neck and over my face.

"Fehling . . . Fischer . . . "

The sergeant gave me a rather quizzical look when I reported my presence later. He nodded condescendingly and looked away as I explained that I stuttered and could not answer when he called my name.

Time pressure, the necessity of giving a specific verbal response, the aura of military authority—all those factors made my stuttering even worse in that R.O.T.C. roll-call situation. At the next assembly, I was made the company guidon bearer; since I would be highly visible in front of the ranks, they wouldn't have to call my name.

Gratefully, that sergeant had not asked me to say my most feared words, my own name. In fact, I found it so difficult to say "Lon Emerick" that I often identified myself as "Bob Nolan" or "Arthur Pendragon" simply because I could say those names. At least I could say them until, slowly, apprehension began to creep into the utterance of those names, too. It was all very confusing: some people knew me as Lon, others as Bob, some as Arthur; a few bewildered souls knew me by more than one of those three names.

Why couldn't I just go ahead and talk? Why did my mouth freeze into such grotesque positions? Why did my jaw gyrate out of control? Why was talking—which even young children can do—such a fearsome task? Did I have some sort of grave neurological or emotional anomaly? What the heck was wrong with me anyway?

My college years were not *all* anger and regret. Far from it. It was at Michigan State University (then still a college) in 1950 that I first experienced profound intellectual stimulation. I'll never forget the intense excitement I felt when I encountered open stacks in the university library. In my typical Celtic excess, I roamed the aisles, flitting from philosophy to forestry in a single ecstatic embrace. It was like walking down a dim corridor and suddenly a door opens, flooding the hallway with light; then another door springs open and another and another. I actually conspired to get locked in the library overnight and then, when detected in the stacks at closing time, had to talk my way out of trouble using my best Jimmy Stewart befuddled impression.

Despite my best efforts to keep it under control in this new college environment, my habit of trying to make people laugh emerged from time to time. Finally, in an introductory biology class one morning, an errant comment convinced me finally to put away such childish things. Picture it: a large class of sleepy freshmen slumped in a huge amphitheater lecture hall. Knowing he would have to capture the attention of the restive collegians right away, the professor patrolled the well of the hall with great wit and flair. He waited until the students were assembled before he made a dramatic entrance with some colorful visual aid or shocking opening statement. And Dr. Gordon was impressive in his long white lab coat, which he always wore over his street clothes.

One morning in late October, as we were beginning a unit on human reproduction, he strode purposefully into the room holding aloft a clear glass bottle with an object immersed in liquid. Walking close to the front row of students, he held the specimen even higher. His other hand was in the pocket of the immaculate white coat. Clearing his throat for attention, he pronounced in his stentorian voice, "In my hand I hold a diseased penis." In the hushed silence that followed (this was, after all, the 1950s)—exactly what the professor had counted on for dramatic effect—I could not help it, it just slipped out. In a clear, fluent response I said, "What you got in the bottle, Doc?"

The hysterical laughter of my fellow students went on and on; class was over for the day and I had learned that fluent speech in the wrong context could also get me into serious trouble.

It has always amazed me that at crucial epochs in my life, a mentor appears to offer wise counsel and encouragement. Not long after I made a shambles of the biology class, I made a connection with Dr. George Wallace, a renowned authority in the study of birds. Dr. Wallace convinced me to take his introductory course in ornithology and, in his intuitive and kindly way, challenged me to share my hopes and aspirations. I was deeply moved when he invited me to join him and a group of colleagues and graduate students for a bird survey.

Dr. Wallace even rescued me when I was arrested—the campus security officer insisted that I was not arrested, merely detained—while training my binoculars on a Blackburnian warbler in a conifer tree. At 5:30 in the morning. Outside a girls' dormitory. When the officer "detained" me I was so upset that I stuttered severely and could not explain my activity. Assured by my obvious nervousness that he had apprehended a real sex deviate, the officer agreed only reluctantly to contact Dr. Wallace when I finally managed to gurgle out his name. When the officer released me, he winked, and affecting a British accent, advised me to look for "birds" in a different locale.

I learned a lot about birds from George Wallace but his research on pesticides and robins opened an entire new world of environmental concerns for me. During three summer vacations from college, I worked as a tree trimmer in Birmingham, Michigan, a wealthy suburb of Detroit. In the mid 1950s, Dutch elm disease was devastating city trees all across the east and midwest. In a panic, Birmingham officials turned to a new compound, dichloro-diphenyl-trichloroethane, which later became infamous as DDT. We sprayed the pesticide continuously, always at night to avoid traffic and ensure calm winds. The DDT was mixed with oil and sprayed in a mist to cover the entire tree and stick to all the leaves and twigs. The mixture stuck to everything—cars, street lights, children's toys; it dripped down on the grass, leaves and soil in flower beds. And on us. The pesticide was safe, we were told, and we wore little or no protection. Little did we know that we were doing a dangerous dance with an elixir of death and that, many years later, it would come back to haunt me.

Dr. Wallace was supervising a research investigation on robins when he and his assistants started finding dead and dying robins all over the campus. Postmortem examinations revealed very high concentrations of DDT in the birds' fat cells. What was happening?

Exploring further, Wallace found that DDT drifted down in the soil from the University's Dutch elm spraying program. Earthworms ingested the pesticide-laden soil and robins then ate the worms. The researchers showed that eating only eleven worms was a lethal dose for the unsuspecting birds. Ominously, it was discovered that DDT becomes even more concentrated as it travels up the food chain; large avian predators like bald eagles and peregrine falcons were rendered unable to reproduce and their numbers declined dramatically. Many observers asked, "What are we doing to the planet?"

George Wallace's robins, along with other research at the time, led to a monumental book, a volume that shocked the world into considering the consequences of toxins being introduced into the environment. In many ways, *Silent Spring* by Rachel Carson was the book which launched the modern environmental movement.

Dr. Wallace, the messenger of bad news, was vilified by the Agriculture and Chemistry Departments as an alarmist, but he lived long enough to be vindicated a decade later when DDT was officially banned in the United States. As young persons are sometimes wont to do, I never properly thanked him at the time for the sensitive impact he had on my life. Years later, as my wife, twin daughters and I hiked along a remote beach of Lake Michigan, we happened upon Doctor and Mrs. Wallace looking for migrant shorebirds. Impulsively, I ran up to him, grasped him in a bearhug and twirled around while offering a long-pent up, emotional thank-you. At first he didn't recognize me. I had changed much from the callow sophomore he knew while he looked just the same and was mildly alarmed at this sudden and emotional embrace. Once I showed him a bit of my residual speech disfluency, he hugged me in return and we held a great reunion.

The rest of my educational experience, however, was not as inspiring and helpful as my mentoring relationship with Dr. Wallace. Finally an event occurred which, although painful to recall, stimulated me to again seek help for my tangled tongue.

A professor asked me to help him put on a demonstration about speech handicaps for a graduate class. Although the thought of talking in front of a group of people—of doing any talking, for that matter—filled me with dread, I did not feel I could refuse his appeal. He was the instructor in a basic course in psychology I was taking and, like so many speech-disabled individuals, I was anxious to gain some measure of acceptance by the normal-talking majority. Perhaps, I convinced myself, I could show the class that stutterers are just average persons who happen to speak in a halting manner. I had no idea what was in store for me.

It turned out to be a "Dog and Pony Show." Like a chief resident physician making rounds with a group of new interns, the professor "presented" me to the students. He lectured at some length about the cause of stuttering. He said he believed that the disorder was rooted in early maternal rejection and that stutterers were orally fixated due to inadequate breast feeding. All the while I stood awkwardly in front of the class. The professor then asked me to state my name and hometown and to identify the residence hall in which I lived. As I tried to respond, the instructor directed the students to observe my lips and mouth.

"Note the symbolic nipple-sucking postures," he said, as I struggled to say my name. Humiliated and outraged, but verbally impotent, I fled the seminar room.

I remember running blindly out of the building, across a wide lawn and down a steep embankment to the river which flowed through the campus. Standing beside the Red Cedar river, I thought momentarily of drowning my stuttering forever in the murky brown water. But then, forsaking self-pity, I walked as fast as I could to the university speech clinic. To my everlasting good fortune, the clinic secretary, upon hearing me try to express my purpose, ushered me into the small office of a newly-appointed faculty member. Ralph Leutenegger had just joined the staff after completing his doctorate under Wendell Johnson, a recovered stutterer and internationally recognized expert on the disorder. Dr. Leutenegger served as my guide for the next three years as I learned how to express myself rather than go by freight.

Initially I expected sympathy, perhaps mixed with a bit of dismay over the severity of my stuttering. Instead, Ralph sat and listened quietly to my long tale of woe. Occasionally he seemed to stutter along with me. When he first did this, I thought he was mocking my grotesque postures and my chest tightened in a surge of anger.

"I'm trying to feel in my own speech musculature," he explained, "how and where you are sticking."

I relaxed a bit but looked at him incredulously.

"You must get acquainted with what you are doing when you stutter," he continued. "Tell me—better yet, show me—where you are tensing and freezing your lips and jaw. Where are you locking up? Until we know precisely what you are doing, we won't know what to alter."

"What the hell is this," I thought, "Where am *I* locking up? For God's sake, stuttering just grabs my words—I cannot open my mouth!"

Almost as if he had read my mind, the speech pathologist persisted in directing me to examine my behavior. His objective scrutiny was infectious. He was the first person I encountered who was willing to examine my stuttering without flinching or recoiling; moreover, he was willing to touch it with his own mouth and talk about it openly. He *wanted* me to stutter so that we would have samples to analyze. My panic began to subside.

"You've got to see that stuttering is your own behavior," Dr. Leutenegger counseled, "and that it's self-defeating. Let's try the *w* sound. How do you say the word 'west'?"

I tried to say "west" and was immediately caught in a long block on the *w*.

"See," he said, as we both watched in a mirror, "you are trying to make the *w* with your mouth wide open. It can't be done. Watch me say 'west'. Notice the difference?"

Damn, damn, damn! There I was, mouth agape, trying to say a sound, *w*, which requires pursed lips. The old conductor's wry joke hit me like a bolt of lightning: I was trying to go by freight when I talked. Right then I began to realize that I was getting in my own way. I had met the enemy and he was me!

Later in that first session, Dr. Leutenegger had me feel my stuttering blocks and listen to them on a recorder; I even managed to duplicate a few voluntarily. When he looked at his watch and announced that he was late for class, I did not want to leave.

"Look," he explained, "stuttering is a verb, not a noun. It's something you *do*, not something that happens to you. It's a set of habits which you have come to believe help you talk."

"WWWWWWWhat do-do yyyyyou mmmmmean?" I asked.

"How can you go ahead and talk when at the same time you are holding back so desperately?" he replied. "All the things you do to try to prevent or stop stuttering, all the tensing and forcing, those things are the stuttering. What you have to do—and it will take some time and considerable energy—is learn to do your stuttering simply and easily."

"BBBBBut IIIIII wwwwant to sssstop sssstuttering! I wailed."

"Sure," Dr. Leutenegger responded. "But you have tried that approach and the problem only got worse. If you aim for an effortless, forward-moving type of disfluency, you will be better served."

Picking up a folder from his desk, Dr. Leutenegger opened the door of his office.

"Here," he said, turning back, "your mental circuits are overloaded right now. Take a coffee break and then look up this reference in the university library. I have it on reserve."

I could not sit still long enough to drink coffee, so I ran immediately to the library. Finding the book, *People in Quandaries* by Wendell Johnson, I turned quickly to the chapter on stuttering titled "The Indians Have No Word For It." It reinforced everything Dr. Leutenegger had said. I remember vividly the growing excitement with which I read that chapter; no other writing has influenced my life so dramatically. This passage in particular, from page 453, is locked into my memory banks:

> "Simple hesitancy in speech is normal and harmless. But to *hesitate to hesitate* (italics mine) is relatively serious in its consequences."

Normally, talking requires little conscious effort and is rarely preplanned; a person simply starts speaking and monitors his performance in an ongoing fashion. It's all pretty automatic, but not for the stutterer. Perhaps this earthy analogy will describe what I am talking about:

The difference between nonstuttering and stuttering speech is like the difference between walking through a dairy cow pasture during the day and at night.

I discovered that I tiptoed through speech—backing up, tensing, speeding up suddenly, avoiding certain words, creating enormous mental barriers. For the next several months I tore into therapy; in my intense drive for relief, I wore out several student speech clinicians. I demanded hard, gritty work and they gave it to me. How sweet it was, as gradually I learned to stutter in open, easy ways. Instead of locking into fixed postures, I learned to slide into feared words. The anxiety, the shame and embarrassment, the frustration, all the negative emotions faded away. I was free, free at last, Lord God almighty, free at last!

I was incredibly lucky. I met the right therapist with the right therapy at the right time. The riddle of stuttering was solved for me. The year of 1953 was the year of my rebirth—I was born again in the sense that I regained membership in the human tribe of talkers. And, oh, did I make up for those lost years! I took courses in public speaking, acted in a play, entered a poetry reading contest. Most of all, I talked—constantly. No one is quite so verbose as a recovered stutterer.

In the midst of all my verbal indulgence, I began to think about how I might repay the wondrous gift of free and easy communication. How could I possibly express my gratitude to the many persons who had helped me? How could I fulfill the obligation I felt toward the field of speech therapy for illuminating the stepping stones to my personal freedom?

I asked Dr. Charles Van Riper, mentor, speech clinician and prodigious author. "I'm so grateful for all that you and others have done to help me,"

I said. "How can I ever repay all of you?" His response was characteristically simple and direct. "Return the deed," he replied. So, after flirting briefly with a career in fisheries and wildlife, I finally did enroll in a program leading to a degree in speech and hearing therapy.

I made a solemn vow unto a sycamore tree that, now I had some freedom of the tongue, I would never again keep silent when I had something to contribute. For too long I had pretended not to know answers in class or allowed others to poke fun at me without responding. I would not go back gently into that dark web of silence.

It is embarrassing to recall, but I must admit that I got carried away with my new found fluency and yielded to the impulse to strike out with speech. I'm chagrined to reveal that I became an intellectual sadist for a time; fuzzy thinking or inadequate preparation was attacked with my new weapon. Fellow students, even faculty members, became targets of opportunity. I didn't realize until much later that I was ventilating a lot of stored up anger. When someone goes through a significant life change, there is always upheaval and estrangement. This rebound behavior, particularly when directed toward my university professors, did not bode well for academic success; I was delayed in earning graduate degrees until I learned to play the apprentice scholar game.

Then, thanks again to the blessing of sweet unbidden providence, goodness and rapture arrived unexpectedly: I met my future life partner; a woman who would love and cherish me unconditionally.

Maxim #2 *Don't Pole Vault Over Mouse Turds*

It is foolish, as well as futile, to expend $20 worth of adrenaline on a 20¢ problem. The Greek stoic philosopher Epictetus observed in the first century that individuals are disturbed not by things but by their opinions of things. In other words, how we feel is dependent upon how we think.

When I get into a circumstance where I may start to overreact, I try to ask myself: If I get upset, will that help the situation? It is liberating to realize that I have a choice, that I am in charge and responsible for my emotional reactions.

I am not advocating a totally detached or passive approach to life–there are too many causes worthy of all our energy, emotional as well as intellectual. What I am saying is: Pick your fights, decide deliberately what events are important in your life. Clearly, burned toast or being cut off in traffic do not require tempestuous responses.

Prize Those Times When You Are Thwarted or Frustrated

The first thing one notices when taking classes in speech therapy is the abundance of women. Attractive, genuine, nurturing women. In my very first course were 29 women—and me. For a socially starved stutterer, it was a veritable heaven; I was a curiosity as well as a classmate. They all wanted to work with me to gain insight and experience into the mysterious and confusing disorder of stuttering. What could I do? So, purely in the interest of furthering their education, I enrolled in therapy each semester. Thus commenced my long, very satisfying and rewarding tenure in the company of women. And what a difference this decades-long association has made in my outlook and in my life.

A fellow student, Joann Anders, slightly older and a whole lot wiser, helped temper my tendency to skewer others with verbal slings and arrows. Her sensitive approach to people served as a perfect counterpoint to the excesses of my newfound communicative freedom. She showed me by example that love and compassion are essential ingredients, perhaps *the* essential ingredients, in being a successful speech therapist.

One day after a seminar in which I had challenged all the students, Joann said quietly, "My granddaddy in West Virginia always told me that 'you can catch more flies with honey than you can with vinegar.' " But Joann also granted me the most important boon of my life: she introduced me to my future wife and played the role of Yenta the Matchmaker with grace and sly humor.

Among the many lovely ladies in the speech therapy program at Michigan State, I found two seniors especially appealing. Margaret was a pony-tailed blonde, cute and bubbling with energy. I liked her and she was fun to talk with but my heart skipped a beat or two when I was around her friend, Lynn McGlothlin. Svelte, attractive, with a halo of honey brown hair, she was very bright, sensitive and possessed a lively spirit. I was smitten. The clincher was that Lynn lived in the Upper Peninsula of Michigan, the site of my Cornish ancestral home, a place I hungered to visit and perhaps live some day.

Joann invited me to dinner with her family and suggested I bring a date. When I showed up with Lynn, Joann was very surprised. She thought I would have the perky blonde in tow. She told me later that she had secretly wished that Lynn and I would get together and she was very pleased with my choice. That dinner party inaugurated a whirlwind courtship and three weeks later, Lynn and I were engaged. It was far and away the best life-decision I ever made.

I floated through the rest of the school year in a state of rapture. Much later, when our daughters reached dating age, they asked how I knew so swiftly that their mother was the one for me. After some broad hints that they should be sure to take more time in such important matters, I gave them a line from an old song by the Platters: "Something deep inside could not be denied." Quite simply, I was incomplete without the Scottish lass from the Upper Peninsula.

It was very difficult to leave Lynn that summer before our marriage to be a therapist at Shady Trails, a camp for young men and boys with stuttering and other communicative disorders. John Clancy, himself a stutterer, founded the camp in the 1930s. At the time I went there in 1958, the camp was administered by the University of Michigan. Despite my loneliness, that summer at Shady Trails was a pivotal clinical experience for me, a time when I focused on the treatment of stutterers and solidified a lifework decision that would last for thirty years and lead to professional success and recognition.

Situated on a beautiful stretch of Lake Michigan shoreline just north of Traverse City, Shady Trails Camp was an idyllic spot to spend a summer. Each June more than 100 boys and young men, the majority of them stutterers, came to the camp for an eight-week intensive residential treatment program. The campers were divided by age into groups of sixteen and housed together in cabins with a counselor and two speech therapists. Every aspect of every day was designed to be therapeutic. From the seven a.m. wake up call until lights out at 9:30 in the evening, we lived, ate, worked and played together. The camp had strong traditions, annual events and songs which united the entire group into a single mind and purpose. Leaving the campers and staff when the camp session ended in mid-August was a very emotional event, even though I was going to be married the next day.

The separation angst vanished as soon as I crossed the newly-constructed Mackinac Bridge; I knew that this wild and beautiful land was where I had to be.

Lynn and I were married on August 17, 1958 in her hometown of Manistique. Her maternal roots go back deeply in this small village on the north shore of Lake Michigan. William S. Crowe, her grandfather, came to this remote spot during the famous white pine lumbering era in the late 1800s and remained to eventually become president of the lumber company and a local bank, as well as an insurance broker and raconteur.

After a brief honeymoon in the Copper Country of the Keweenaw Peninsula, a rocky finger of land jutting out into Lake Superior, we pooled our meager belongings and headed to East Lansing to begin our life together. How excited we were to move into a brand-new apartment in Spartan Village, a housing complex for married students! I remember fondly the three years we spent at Michigan State University. While there are always bumps in the road when two lives are merged, we were deeply committed to each other. We worked things out. Even our diurnal differences. I am a lark. I awaken early, full of energy and eager to greet the day. Lynn, of course, is an owl (larks always marry owls) and her metabolism warms up more slowly; she is going strong in the evening when I am ready to crash. The lark must learn not to sing near the owl in the morning, especially if he keeps repeating fragments of songs over and over.

Although we had little money, we both enjoyed the outdoors and spent considerable time roaming the university wood lots and nearby parks. A big date for us consisted of attending the university-sponsored travelogues. Tickets were only 50 cents and we could splurge on a milkshake after the show. But mostly we studied.

As a first year speech therapist in several local schools, Lynn was very busy. She carried a large caseload of children and spent time each evening preparing lesson plans and devising materials to use in her therapy sessions. I kept up with graduate classes, wrote several papers and fulfilled my duties as a graduate assistant in the speech therapy department. Together, we finished my Master's thesis; I wrote, Lynn typed.

My research project involved testing attitudes of teachers toward stuttering. To one group of subjects I was supposed to introduce the task with stuttered speech; I could do that with little problem. However, the control group portion of the study required that I read the instructions fluently.

Ah, there was the rub. The nemesis of stuttering is the desire to be totally fluent, to conceal stuttering at any cost. It is a very slippery slope because it leads to avoidances, subterfuge, increased tension and, inevitably, more stuttering. I knew that if I slipped and spoke with disfluency, the data would be useless. While I managed to read the instructions perfectly, the strain aggravated old fears and triggered the return of old habits. One night shortly after the research presentations, I hesitantly told Lynn I thought I was beginning to stutter again. She responded without looking up from her lesson plans, "Well, it's a good thing you know what to do about it." This is typical of her clear thinking. She cuts through all the balderdash to the core of an issue. Right, I thought. I did know what to do about it.

Without pausing, I moved from the Master's to a doctoral program. I knew by then that I wanted to teach at a university and the Ph.D. degree is the required union card for entering this august domain. The necessary course work was completed quickly. I even passed the French exam—fulfilling the archaic academic requirement which demanded a reading fluency in one foreign language—by reverting to my trickster/comedian past. When I flunked the French test the first time, I noted the examiner, an elderly woman, supplied words for me whenever I exhibited even a mild stuttering. So when I returned to retake the language examination, I purposely stuttered whenever I was unsure of the translation, and the same lady filled in the words for me. I passed.

Now, lest the reader be too judgmental about my ploy, remember that listeners had gratuitously supplied words for me for many years. A person who stutters hates this; even though it may provide temporary relief from frustration when someone blurts out the message he is trying to say, in the long run it exacerbates the problem by creating dependence. Anyway, I figure the French test evened the score.

Even though I had calmed considerably from my stuttering-rebound-intellectual-terrorist period, I still had trouble suffering nitwits gladly. Dealing with the blatant gamesmanship of my faculty dissertation committee was excruciating. The professors were all members of the Ph.D. fraternity and tradition calls for a requisite amount of hazing before newcomers are admitted to the ranks. I knew how to play the game: Jump dutifully through all the hoops while chanting, "Yes, doctor. Very good suggestion, doctor. Thank you, doctor." After years of being a silent second-class citizen, I could not, or perhaps would not, genuflect to the academic rituals.

The situation came to a volatile impasse when my advisor, chairman of the committee, nixed a dissertation topic he had previously approved and on which I had spent seven months researching and writing a lengthy proposal. Inspecting his marginal notes on a copy of the proposal, it was clear to me that the chairman did not understand the background research; all he had done was highlight some grammatical errors and changed all my uses of "which" to "that." I made some intemperate remark in a meeting and, like muskoxen, the five other committee members circled the chairman and closed ranks. I had violated the rules of the game. It would take five years, more maturity on my part, and the resignation of the troglodyte dissertation advisor, before I would finish the doctoral degree.

But every crisis offers an opportunity. We decided to obtain some distance from the distasteful dissertation barrier and enter the then wide-open job market. Sight unseen, I was hired to develop a brand-new speech therapy program at a small college in western Minnesota. It was here at the little college on the prairie that it became apparent that I was an unusually gifted teacher. In the words of the Bard, "Sweet are the uses of adversity."

Maxim # 3 ***Prize those times when you are thwarted or frustrated***

Cherish the experience of being blocked for it may well be a disguised opportunity for growth. If you learn to accept, even embrace, the awkward and the difficult, then you are on the leading edge of creativity. Struggle is the law of growth and when someone is challenged, he or she must learn new strategies. Difficulty is a normal, maybe even a necessary, part of life; if you have no times of doubt, no anxious moments, maybe the task is not worth doing.

I used to tell students during their supervised therapy practice that if they did not make some mistakes, they weren't pushing the envelope hard enough. If you go through life thinking about all the bad things that could happen, you soon convince yourself to do nothing.

Changing, altering old and comfortable habits, is very difficult. Habits are like fences: while they may protect us from possible danger, they also keep us confined within certain limiting boundaries. Rarely does someone change anything substantive about himself unless he undergoes some significant emotional experience. The emotional event shatters the person's typical ways of perceiving and behaving; it creates such an upheaval that even very old patterns of behavior are no longer appropriate or useful. Like the crustacean which must shed its protective shell in order to grow, there is always risk and vulnerability when humans undertake a new challenge.

Let me say it a different way: The person has to be emotionally receptive to change. You cannot simply reason a person out of a position they have not reasoned themselves into.

The way in which we confront barriers will determine whether we are chronically thwarted or see frustration as a challenge to forge new levels of understanding and skill.

Some individuals focus narrowly on the problem. I was always surprised by the number of my colleagues in the academic arena, where new ideas are supposed to be venerated, who approached each problem situation from the vantage point of negativity. Most of us have attended meetings where some participants seem to delight in telling others why nothing can be done. "Oh, we can't do that because..." or "Yes, but..." Beware of the 'yes, but' persons in your life for they will drain your creative energy which may be what they intend. These negative nabobs stress the magnitude of the barrier, how difficult or even impossible it is to even promote a solution. When anyone suggests a way to deal with the problem, the problem-oriented members cite all the reasons why it will not work.

How much better it is to work with a person who focuses on solutions, someone who acknowledges that the problem exists but suggests ways of solving it. In my life, and in my clinical work, I always found that from a small covey of promoted solutions, there emerges a tentative plan, an embryonic design of getting around, over or under the barrier.

Whenever I accepted a new client for stuttering therapy, I was immediately assailed by doubts and an overwhelming sense of responsibility. But then I always remembered my own poor prognosis many decades ago. I had received therapy from more than a dozen therapists and failed twelve times to conquer my stuttering nemesis. Like Sisyphus, who was condemned to roll up a hill a huge stone which constantly rolled back, I came close to the promised land of speech free from disfluency several times, only to relapse badly. It took a traumatic emotional turmoil for me finally to commit totally to change.

And what a difference a few months make! For the first 20 years of my life, all the pain and frustration emanated from stuttering. Then the evil was transformed into a shining gift. Because of stuttering, I met my Life Partner, have two beautiful and creative daughters, a host of clients and students who enriched my days, some professional success and recognition, and a life of joy and exploration beyond any youthful expectations.

Surely only a fool would batter his life energy against a granite barrier, and the individual who is chronically frustrated would no doubt profit from some counseling. But to eschew all tasks that seem difficult, to deny yourself the opportunity to accomplish mighty deeds by taking prudent risks is a sadly limiting way to pass through this marvelous life. Theodore Roosevelt's credo put it this way:

> "Far better it is to dare mighty things, to win glorious triumphs, even though checkered by failure, than to take rank with those poor spirits who neither enjoy much nor suffer much, because they live in a gray twilight that knows not victory nor defeat."

DON'T WEAR A RAINCOAT IN THE SHOWER

The first day of a new class in a new semester was still, even in the twilight of my teaching career, a magical event. The potential is exciting beyond description: What will happen in the next four months? What will I discover about my students and myself as we explore and stretch our minds? The classroom always crackles with energy and exhilaration on this first day.

Now was the time to pass along the lamp of learning to younger hands. So, after our first class, I took my graduate assistant for coffee in the student union so I could outline her responsibilities during the semester. I had known Diane since she was a freshman and during her undergraduate years she had taken several classes from me. We also had shared several clinical experiences, one where she had worked brilliantly with a severe adult stutterer. Together with other students, we had hiked, snowshoed and enjoyed cookouts at my cabin. We were close. Now as I opened the class folder to retrieve some materials, I noticed she was staring at me over her coffee mug with a curious facial expression.

"What?" I asked, smiling at her wry grin. She remained silent.

"What!?" I asked again in mock exasperation.

"I've finally figured it out," Diane responded after a lengthy pause.

"What?" I asked more insistently, my curiosity piqued.

"After all those courses I took from you, I think I finally figured how what you do when you teach," she responded. "I never realized it until today when I was observing, you know, objectively as a teaching assistant."

"What . . . ?" I repeated laughingly.

Diane paused to take a sip of coffee and collect her thoughts. "You weave a spell around your students . . . they are mesmerized," she said. "I mean, you put them in a comfort zone so they are psychologically ready to learn." Diane looked out the window for a moment and then continued. "You make learning fun—no anxiety, no tedium."

"Aw, shucks, a ma'am," I joked, hanging my head like an embarrassed cowboy. "It tain't nothin'."

Diane's comments started me thinking about the early years as a new college teacher at Moorhead State. I had always avoided analyzing my teaching prowess, fearing that if I tried to pick it apart, I might not be able to put it back together again. It seemed like a magical gift and I feared that rational scrutiny would somehow destroy the magic. But after saying goodbye to Diane, I was strangely restless. So overcome was I by recollections of years long gone that I had to take a saunter on campus and surrender to the glorious memories which spilled into my consciousness.

Every university professor is entitled to at least one Camelot in his or her teaching career. I was blessed with three: Moorhead State College, Northern Michigan University, and then an unexpected coda at Northern Arizona University.

But the first Camelot is always the best. In 1961 we moved to Moorhead, Minnesota to begin a thirty-year tenure in the academic world. What a colorful caravan we made motoring across Michigan, Wisconsin and Minnesota with a maroon car, topped by a red Old Town canoe and hauling an orange rental trailer.

Moorhead is located in northwestern Minnesota just across the Red River from its twin city of Fargo, North Dakota. This is open, flat prairie. As far as a person can see in any direction—and one can see a long, long way—there are open plains; this area is the lake bed of the once immense glacial Lake Agassiz. The rich soil is incredibly fertile and produces bumper harvests of sugar beets and other crops. We were unsettled by the open horizons, the constant wind and the absence of trees. When we were sent to inspect a rental house, the realtor said to go north from town and turn left at the cottonwood tree in the field. For two lovers of the forest, this direction-by-the-lone-tree was a disconcerting and yet somewhat humorous experience.

When I related our experience to a colleague, he chuckled and said, "You gotta love this town . . . look at this headline." When the settlers first came to this region, they were so impressed by the rich agricultural land, they named several villages in grateful celebration. Just north of Moorhead were two such hamlets, one named Climax and the other Fertile. In bold black print, the newspaper proclaimed: *Fertile Woman Dies in Climax.*

We spent four wonderful years in Moorhead. We liked the warm, open people we met, cherished the students who flocked to a new banner of learning and gradually came to admire the long vistas the prairie offers.

I was hired to initiate a four-year educational curriculum leading to a B.A. degree in speech therapy. Moorhead State College (now University) was then a small state-supported institution with a main mission of training public school teachers. About 2000 students were enrolled in the fall semester when I took up my new duties as an assistant professor.

How youthful, naive and confident I was (only one thing has changed over the years) as I set out to accomplish what I was sure were going to be mighty deeds. I would teach all of the courses, develop and supervise an active clinic for student practicum and do demonstration therapy myself. I was full of pent-up energy from years as a stutterer and then as a subjugated doctoral candidate.

In retrospect, I'm a bit chagrined at the wide swath I made through that small college. On the first day of class registration, I noticed a young man sitting on the steps of Old Main. He looked glum as he filled out several forms in preparation for enrollment. Stopping to get directions, I asked him how things were going. Dave was a senior majoring in secondary education and it soon became apparent that he was disenchanted with the curriculum and his prospects for the future.

"Would you like to be a pioneer?" I asked and then explained what I had been hired to do. Dave was my first major in speech therapy. Soon he brought in several of his fraternity brothers who had heard Dave's excited descriptions of the new curriculum. The program grew like Topsy.

From the first moment I entered the classroom, I knew that this was my realm. This was my calling. It sounds incredibly self-serving, I know, but I was convinced that not only was I going to be a good teacher, I was going to be a great, even legendary, teacher.

My teaching style flowed from my essence, from a very personal well-spring, not from any formal training. I am happy to say I took no courses in how to teach. My approach was strictly intuitive and spontaneous. I never planned or even really knew what twists and turns I would take during a class.

Only many years later, long after I had retired from the university and gone on to the next chapter in life, did I come to understand the basis for my success as a teacher. Scores of former students, some themselves now university professors, wrote to tell me how I had inspired and challenged them. I'm not perceptive enough to identify every facet of my teaching style, but comments from my students and colleagues seemed to repeatedly focus on three elements: *enthusiasm, organization* and *humanity* liberally spiced with humor.

The students all remember my *enthusiasm* as infectious. Let me confess it: I had the best job in the world—and it showed. I got to share issues and ideas about very important human problems; I was privileged to spend my days with spirited young people; I was encouraged, even supported, to pursue my scholarly interests. Sometimes I felt that I should pay the university for this wonderful outlet for my passion.

I was ecstatic about my work; I believed, I still believe, that I was given a mission to fulfill and I could hardly wait to get to class. In fact, I always arranged to get there early so I could chat with students and focus my mind on the impending presentation. My students reported that they saw a person totally enthralled with his topic and that they were inspired to learn and grow without realizing they were being swept up in the classroom energy and momentum. They, too, came to believe that they were chosen to share the mission of bringing help to the speech disabled.

Without *organization*, in the absence of carefully delineated objectives for learning, enthusiasm or good intentions yield little except undirected arousal. This is comparable to a mobile ice cream vendor patrolling a suburban street with an empty truck. Each semester, I gave the students an extensive syllabus which spelled out the concepts we would focus upon. I insisted that they keep notes in their own language, use their own analogies; I often would stop in mid-phrase and ask them to rephrase what I had just said. Assignments were designed to sharpen their awareness, challenge them to seek patterns and strive to distill the essence of the issue under study.

The compulsive organization I used in presenting materials became an ongoing joke. Often, I abandoned a concept to relate some long clinical anecdote and then, trying to get back on track, I would ask, "Let's see, are we on A, under I or II?" In order to keep my lectures fresh and alive, I discarded the class folder every year or so and started over again.

But the students maintained that it was my *humanity* and sense of humor which made the classes so appealing. Whenever someone asked me what subject area I taught, I always responded that I teach students not subject matter. I was not trying to be coy; I sincerely believe that you make people grow by building fires inside them, not under them. My job was to create novel and exciting learning experiences so that the students would strive and seek for personal understanding.

For example, I insisted that each student, working in pairs to enhance observation, go into the local community and stutter noticeably in three social situations. The students hated and loved this assignment. The hardest part was taking the initial plunge, to enter a store or office and reveal themselves to be communicatively different. But the insights they acquired from this hands-on experience were monumental. Not only did they come to understand in a small way what it is like to be a stutterer—and thus be better able to say to a future client, "I know how you feel"—they also witnessed the insensitivity of most listeners toward persons who speak with a slow and halting tongue. Once, when four pairs of student therapists went into the same large store, one after the other, the manager asked the final two students, "Are you people holding a convention in town?"

Incidentally, however, our efforts paid off in another way: The local business community became interested in how to be better listeners for their speech-disabled customers.

Remembering how important it was in my own life when a few professors stepped away from their professional status and offered me a person-to-person relationship, I strived to make myself accessible and open to my students. I made it a point to learn their names, their hometowns and something else about them. On the first day of class I asked them each to fill out a small card and include a note on what item they would leave on their desk to represent themselves if they were absent for the day.

The students knew that I cared about them as people. My assumption was that no one cares what you know until they know that you care. And not one student took advantage of my personalized approach in thirty years of university teaching. Well, now that I think about it, one student did call me at home one night and said that if I didn't change his grade from a C to an A, he would be subject to the draft and sent to Vietnam. I didn't and he wasn't.

Humor has always been a large part of my persona and it was simply natural for me to assume the role of an educational entertainer. My classes were filled with gaiety. I firmly believe that in order to engage higher cortical brain activity, you must first turn on lower-level activating centers. I decided right at the outset that I wanted to break up the class-going note-taking routine so typical of many course offerings. So I disarmed the students with funny anecdotes. Questions using students' names and current events were hidden among the real questions on exams. The students were always on edge, attentively wondering when the next stunt, the next bit of hilarity would occur.

I was astounded at how the students rallied to the banner of speech therapy at Moorhead State. Amazingly, the students did the recruiting. They apparently spread the word so well about the new wild and crazy professor that their friends and roommates starting coming to my classes. Imagine, a college student coming to a class in which she is not enrolled!

The speech therapy program ballooned to 34 majors in the second semester of its initiation. I was overrun with therapy, teaching and the administrative details which university departments so cherish. The students would drop by my office on their way for coffee and invite me to join them. When I pointed out the stack of forms I needed to complete, they took off their coats and pitched in to help. We became like a large, energetic family.

The students were almost as excited as the new parents when our lovely twin daughters were born near midnight on January 19, 1964. In that time before current imaging techniques, we didn't know that Lynn was carrying twins; she did suspect there was more than one set of elbows and knees. It was also before the time when fathers were welcome in the delivery room, so I was dismissed to pace restlessly outside in the corridor. When the obstetrician came out a short while later, he announced, "Well, you have the daughter you wanted—in fact, you have two!"

We had only one name selected for a girl—Lynn, like her mom, and decided to name the second little girl Mary after a very special student, Mary Karen Larson. Since our families lived back in Michigan and I could not call them to come and share the event, I phoned a student, Russ, and told him the news. Within 15 minutes, Russ appeared, running down the hall toward the nurses' station. What an apparition he made! A former collegiate wrestler, Russ is a burly six feet two inches. He swept me up in a bearhug, twirled me around and shouted, "You had twins, you had twins!"

The nurses had a hard time calming us down so that we wouldn't disturb other patients on the floor.

I was so wrapped up in my work and family that I didn't notice that some of my colleagues in other departments were not as happy as I was about the growth of the speech therapy program. I guess I was a very callow youth because I thought that faculty members were dedicated to their academic disciplines—thoughtful, chalk-covered creatures whose lives were dominated by inquiry. How would they have time for something as venal as envy? My department chairman, Delmar Hansen, bless his soul, dealt with most of the negative comments. "They say you make learning too easy, the students have too much fun," he reported one day with a broad smile of satisfaction. "The main complaint about your approach is that scholarship should be difficult, tedious, hard won." Some others complained that I was too friendly with the students. In some quarters, I was known as the Pied Piper Professor. "Can you blame them?" Delmar added, "you are luring students away from their departments, and professors patrol their academic boundaries with some zeal. I love it!"

During the fourth year of the Moorhead Camelot, an unexpected opportunity arose to move to our beloved Upper Peninsula of Michigan. How could I leave such a tightknit band of enthusiastic students? It was a difficult decision but we both hungered for the miles of dense forest, the rushing rivers and the immense presence of Lake Superior. To be sure, we had found some outlets for our devotion to nature—Itasca State Park, birthplace of the Mississippi River, and the Boundary Waters Canoe Country—but they were miles away from home.

The decision to accept the new position at Northern Michigan University was almost made by the time I drove the 500 miles from Minnesota to Marquette for an interview. Weary from hours on the road, synapses eroded by traffic, I came over the crest of a hill just west of town and saw Lake Superior framed between rock cuts on either side and stretching out to the horizon. "The Blue Profound," my grandfather always called the big lake. I knew that this was where I wanted, indeed, had to be.

When I told the recruitment committee that I would love to come to Northern, the registrar looked at the dean and with a broad smile, spoke up, "I've had at least a dozen inquiries already from students at Moorhead State College who want to transfer here—I think we're getting a good one, Dean West."

Maxim # 4 ***Don't Wear Your Raincoat In The Shower***

Life, it has been said, is not a dress rehearsal. So when you decide to do something, give it everything you have. Here and now, this is the life we have and the time we are given.

When we don't live fully, when we spend too much mental energy reviewing the past or worrying about the future, we miss the opportunity of the present moment.

Some people talk a good game; they have good intentions but don't translate them into activity. Edward Abbey observed that sentiment without action tends to erode the human spirit. Inaction generalizes to other life enterprises and impairs a person's capacity to make genuine commitments or strive to act upon them. In the lexicon of the street, "They talk the talk, but don't walk the walk."

One of the best ways I know to live fully aware in the present moment is to take a walk in the woods. Try giving yourself up to the forest: focus on what you are seeing, hearing, smelling as you saunter along. If you remember to leave the rest of your world at the trail head, I can guarantee that you will return refreshed.

THE LAW OF THE ECHO

It was the first day of mid-semester vacation and all through the library not a computer was stirring, not even a student was evident. Almost hidden behind a stack of professional journals, I was hard at work on a textbook when a faculty member from a different department stopped by to say hello.

"The university would be a nice place to work if it didn't have all those students lurking about, wouldn't it?" he said, only half in jest. I smiled a bit at this arcane quip and returned to my labors. There are some faculty members, though, who are serious about it, even while they recognize that without collegians there would be no college.

Actually, I thought afterward while returning to my office, the university would be an abysmal place to work without the students. Who would want to spend his days in the company of unctuous administrators and pedantic academicians? The students make this institution come alive and without their stimulating presence, I would have gone into watch repair or bookkeeping long ago.

There was a brief period when I first came to Northern Michigan University, however, when I did entertain the thought of closing my office door and hiding out from the speech therapy majors. We were developing a new Master's degree program and it entailed endless planning and paperwork to satisfy the standards of a national accrediting body. I was trying to complete a doctoral dissertation at Michigan State University, a task which required frequent trips to East Lansing. Worst of all, I was trying to adapt to being director of the speech therapy program, a job which demanded administrative expertise and attention to university politics, skills in which I was terribly deficient.

Then one day as I filled out yet another form detailing our departmental budget for the financial office, I had a revelation. As they often did throughout the day, a number of students dropped by my office to sit in my rocking chair and schmooze. Irritated more at the task than at the students, I complained to the secretary that all the interruptions were keeping me from my work. Then, as I walked down the hall to fill my coffee cup, it hit me: "These students *are* my work!" That epiphany moved me to abandon the clinic directorship as soon as possible and avoid ever again administrative duties in any form. Fortunately, I had a number of good colleagues who shared my sense of mission.

John Hatten was fresh out of the Ph.D. program at the University of Wisconsin. Young, eager, with a puckish sense of humor, he was an ideal partner to help launch the new Master's degree at Northern. At the time, the mid-1960s, very few of the speech therapists working in the public schools held Master's degrees. The State of Michigan mandated that a worker without an advanced degree must have her caseload certified by someone with at least a Master's degree. John and I traveled throughout the Upper Peninsula helping local therapists evaluate their caseloads and offering them encouragement and support for seeking an advanced degree. We always took some advanced students with us so that they could gain field experience in actual work settings. Those trips were lively with lots of humor, stops for treats and endless talk about our mission in the vineyard of speech therapy.

Both John and I had spouses trained in speech therapy and we each had two young daughters. Our families shared interests in the outdoors and went on many saunters together. I was so impressed with Hatten's organized approach to ideas that later I persuaded him to coauthor a textbook with me. The book was widely adopted and now, 30 years later in its 6th edition, is authored by one of our former students.

John possessed the unusual talent of being able to tap on his teeth with a pencil and, by altering the shape of his mouth, produce a more than passable melody. During boring meetings (a redundancy, I know), it would crack me up to hear the faint rhythms of "Moon River" or "On Top of Old Smoky" coming from John's side of the conference table.

We were blessed also with an exceptional leader. How can I adequately describe the chairman of the speech department, our source of support, encouragement and protection? James Rapport is larger than life. When we broke through a wall to enlarge our cramped quarters in the speech clinic—the national accrediting agency demanded that we have more square footage to gain approval and we had been promised the space for almost a year—Jim galloped to our defense with his extraordinary combination of charm, logic and good humor. Affectionately known as "Daddy Bear" by faculty and students alike, he is an amazingly vital presence.

Trained in the theater and an accomplished actor, Daddy Bear is even better at improvisation than Robin Williams. One time at a retirement dinner party for a prominent local speech therapist, the honored guest droned on and on after she was given an achievement award plaque. Using each initial letter in the word "therapist," she described at length the attributes a therapist must possess. As she reached the letter "P" and delineated in detail the qualities of "presence," "persistence," "patience" and "preparation," Jim leaned over and whispered, "I'm glad she's not an invertebrate palaeontologist."

The chairman understood and endorsed our mission to create the best educational training program for speech therapists in the Upper Midwest. Even when several theater majors changed over to our curriculum, his support never wavered.

We were quite a large band of happy warriors at Northern, marching forth to serve those with speech disorders. I continued my same personal approach to the students as I had at Moorhead. My rationale is simple: The teacher is the students' only familiar face in a new and sometimes arduous experience. I believe that it is very important for the professor to give up some of his traditional authority in exchange for offering collegians his humanity. But this is all post hoc reasoning. At the time I was just being me; I am glad I followed a path less taken in higher education because it has meant all the difference in my own pilgrimage to openness and authenticity. Besides, I had more fun than some of my pompous colleagues. And, as a former student observed when she contacted me recently after a long hiatus, they won't get a phone call twenty years later.

The door to my office was always open when I was there and I furnished the room to be homey and inviting. The students always migrated to the padded rocking chair and delighted in the photographs of my daughters and the small vase of polished Lake Superior stones on a nearby table. I placed my desk against a wall so that it would not be a barrier between me and a visitor.

But the most appealing aspect, according to the many former students who still keep in touch with me, is that I did therapy *with* them.

One of the most onerous tasks in my profession was supervision of student therapists as they learned about the treatment process by working with real clients. For me, the worst part was sitting relatively quiescently in a darkened room, watching the students' efforts through a two-way mirror. And then, after the session was over, offering a critique that would help the beginner improve her performance. It all seemed so passive and feeble to me. So I did therapy with the students in a team-treatment approach.

Long dissatisfied with the conventional treatment of adolescent stutterers—two or three times a week in one hour sessions—I sought a different, more intensive way to counteract the deeply negative communicative environment in which a stutterer lives. Too often I observed that the client would gain some insight and even proficiency in the management of his problem during an hour's clinic session and then would find that implementing these changes in a realistic conversational setting was just too difficult.

Borrowing a page from my pivotal experience at Shady Trails Camp, we created what came to be known as an "intensive therapy weekend." The students called it a "therapy blitzkreig." Generally we commenced the festivities on a Friday afternoon. With all the role playing, trips to real communicative settings in town and group meals, it did take on the qualities of a festival. We worked quite late, sometimes as late as midnight, were back at it all day Saturday and had a final session and celebration at a Sunday brunch.

Sometimes we had several stutterers going through a weekend treatment program together. This always added a dimension to the therapy because we could hold group sessions. As in other disorders, persons who stutter learn a lot by watching and working with each other. The climate in the clinic during these weekend sessions was astoundingly energetic. Out of the seeming chaos emerged a remarkable synthesis of purpose. Here was a team of four to eight students, one or more stutterers and the supervisor all pulling in the same direction. In effect, we created a small society in which stuttering was not only accepted, it was encouraged on the premise that the disorder had to be out in the open before we could change it. Each client could see a monumental change; he could visualize the promised land. Of course, we would have to follow up in the next few weeks, but the response to those blitzkreig sessions was astonishing. And not just for the persons who stuttered. The students saw theory transformed into action and results in three short days. Those intensive weekend therapy sessions were physically exhausting, terribly time-consuming and emotionally draining. I loved them. So did the students. As soon as one session was completed and evaluated, they begin to clamor for another.

As the word spread about our intensive treatment approach, we began to get referrals from all over the United States and several foreign countries. On more than one occasion, we took our stuttering show on the road to other universities. By the time we got back to Marquette, the students were immensely proud of themselves and felt as if they were ten feet tall.

However, I always believed that students are not prepared by information and practicum alone. You don't help people grow only by lecturing them and assigning them lengthy tomes to read or even including them in novel therapy experiences. It is futile to expect that plants or collegians can be made to flourish by pulling at their tops. Instead, you must enrich the learning environment by nourishing the whole person.

As a dedicated disciple of Henry David Thoreau, I naturally wanted to share my affection for woods and waters with my students. Whenever possible, we abandoned the lecture hall and speech clinic for saunters and cookouts in remote places. We played hooky from the university—the statute of limitations has expired so now I can confess—stealing time from our academic and clinical duties for psychic cleansing. The students called these outings "mental hygiene days" and we all rationalized that as laborers in the vineyard of speech therapy we must keep ourselves in better psychological health than our clients.

My colleagues raised their eyebrows—and my guilt level—when they made sly remarks about the "nature boy" and his entourage tramping in the forests. A few bluntly asked, in rhetorical fashion and with a distinct ruffling of their academic feathers, what a sojourn to a spring waterfall had to do with a college education. Perhaps, I worried, I was simply indulging my own need to relate to others in the context of the out-of-doors.

But the students responded to the outings, even to extent of rising before dawn—no small sacrifice for a collegian—to watch a sunrise before we cooked breakfast. A list for the semester's excursions was posted on my office door; the adventures became so popular that we had to limit the number of participants in order to retain the quality of each experience.

It was not difficult to notice changes in the students on these hikes: they seemed more spontaneous, free and open. At first I thought they were simply less guarded outside the formal classroom setting, relating better to the professor as a person without textbooks, tests and other trappings of academe. I am sure that was part of it. But there was more. The students—

even tense, anxious Master's candidates—seemed to relax and visibly grow calm as they sat and watched an open fire or picked their way on snowshoes through a winter forest.

In the process we learned a basic truth: Nature extends wondrous healing powers to those willing to seek its calm. On our woodland sojourns we discovered what Wordsworth meant when he wrote that the earth offers "a presence that disturbs our mind with the joy of elevated thought."

In addition to our outdoor experiences, the students and I met regularly for breakfast at various restaurants in the Marquette area. There was always good wild talk, an abundance of hilarity and sometimes serious discussions about what the future held for them and their chosen field. Together we shared the turmoil of the late 1960s and 1970s. I recall those tumultuous years with fondness. The students were idealistic, totally committed to the improvement of life and zealous in pursuit of goals once you helped them focus their youthful energies. It was great to be around them.

And they liked to be around me. I was not trying to be a peer to the students nor did they ever think of me as a buddy. They knew that my expectations for them were very high. While I always tried to accept and support them in their present level of achievement, I held up an image of what they were capable of becoming. I have never accepted the notion, shared by many of my colleagues at the university, that the professor should be an emotion-free neutral conduit for, as they put it, "pounding the nails of information into the thick skulls of indifference." I demanded excellence, and tried always to model it, but I attempted to balance my demands with an equivalent amount of support.

As I had done so many years before at Michigan State University, the few men enrolled in our speech therapy program relished the abundant female companionship. It was inevitable that I would also play the role of matchmaker for some students. Working closely together in therapy teams and sharing many outdoor adventures, attractions ensued and several blossomed into marriage.

One of the most rewarding matches for our family involved our sometime child-sitter. A sweet Irish lass from the Upper Peninsula with a gorgeous complexion and winning smile, Maureen captivated Bill, a senior who shared my crazy sense of humor and who showed great promise as a scholar and teacher. With our daughters, then five years old, we attended the wedding and shared in their happiness. Now, many years later, Maureen and Bill both hold Ph.D. degrees and teach in a southeastern university. What provocative turns our lives take!

It always overwhelms me when I think of how many lives I have touched—and been touched by—over the years. The only lasting immortality we can have, it seems to me, is through our influence on others. She who I fired with my enthusiasm in turn fires others and the impact, while perhaps diminishing, goes on forever. And in some form, it always comes back.

Maxim #5 ***Remember the Law of the Echo***

Everything we do comes back to us. Our actions start a reaction like the ripples created when a stone is cast into a pond. The ripples move outward in ever larger circles, losing energy to be sure, but also making impacts on others in ways we often cannot know. He whose life I touch, touches others, and like a celestial game of billiards, the energy flows endlessly. Then, when we least expect it, the ripples can reappear on our personal shore in a refreshing eddy, and enrich our lives again.

The law of the echo grants us continuity of our lives in the minds and spirits of others.

An old Cornish proverb: "The heart that gives...gathers."

THERE YOU ARE

Gilles de la Tourette was the furthest thing from my mind as I unlocked the door to the speech clinic and hurried in out of the swirling snow. I had been gone for a week attending the graduation ceremony where I was finally, officially, awarded a doctoral degree, and there was a lot of work piled up. It was only 7:00 a.m. and I would have time to organize for the three classes I had to teach, assemble diagnostic materials for a session with a severe adult stutterer and scan my notes for the thesis committee meeting in the late afternoon. As I rushed down the dimly lit hallway to my office, I almost knocked over a young man pulling a trash bin out of one of the therapy rooms. Before I could excuse myself, he erupted with a series of obscenities.

"Up yours! Up yours!" he yelled in my face.

My mind raced irrationally—I have a brand-new doctorate and I've just been appointed an associate professor.

"Now, wait just a darn min- . . . " I began to respond.

"Fuck you! Smell my dick!" the janitor shouted. Then he did something unexpected that deflated my burgeoning anger: he smiled.

"I'm sorry . . . uk! uk! I have this problem and . . . ," he started to say. I didn't hear the rest of his message because I knew what was happening. The young man, who introduced himself as Jerry, had Tourette's Syndrome, a rare neurological disorder characterized by involuntary movements and explosive, often obscene speech.

My tasks forgotten, I invited Jerry into my office where we talked for almost an hour. A part-time student at Northern, he could get through a class with only minor outbursts; sometimes he would attempt to mask vulgar expressions with coughing. But if the teacher called on him—which they rarely did a second time—he lost control. Holding a job involving meeting the public was very difficult, which is why he was working as a janitor in the early morning hours. Social situations were a real strain.

"I go to the supermarket late at night so I don't offend someone," he said. "There is medication for Tourette's but it makes me feel dopey, like living in a mental fog." Jerry was most upset about his inability to relate to young women. I wrote down exactly what he said about this: "There was a real mixture of conflicting emotions when I began dating. I wanted to go out with girls, to socialize and have a normal relationship. On the other hand, whenever a girl did accept a date with me, especially more than once, I invariably began wondering what was wrong with her—why would she want to go out with *me*?"

I knew that speech therapy has little to offer those with Tourette's Syndrome, yet Jerry's lament moved me deeply that morning, reminding me of my own youthful frustrations as a stutterer dealing with the dating game. Because I understood on a deep and personal level what speech disabled persons were going through, my clients always found it easier to identify with me as a therapist. Although this did provide a distinct advantage in treatment, I tried not to overwork the sharing of my own idiosyncratic struggles. It is too easy to punish others unwittingly for one's own inadequacies or be totally unaware of lingering blind spots. Since most of my clinical work focused upon persons who stutter, I had to be particularly vigilant in all my clinical encounters with my brethren of the tangled tongue.

About 1% of the United States population has a stuttering problem. It's a small and exclusive fraternity; most stutterers are male. I was particularly zealous in trying to limit additional membership in the club of the tangled tongues. Fortunately, the prevention of stuttering in young children is far easier than it is to work with confirmed adult stutterers. If the problem can be caught in time, it can be reversed completely, usually by counseling with the adults in the child's life.

I had to monitor myself carefully when I worked with parents bringing their children to the clinic with fears of beginning stuttering, lest I chastise them for my own parents' handling of my speech problem.

Colin Brannon was three years old when his parents brought him to the speech clinic with the complaint that the child was beginning to stutter. Colin, a precocious tyke with curly blond hair, did have some speech bobbles, but they were brief and he uttered them with little or no tension. The child talked a lot and showed no evidence of fear or frustration. All this was good. Clearly, the child was showing normal developmental speech interruptions, but he was not stuttering. I knew that we could remedy the situation by helping the parents alter their expectations of speech development and thus eliminate their concerns and attempts at home remedies. But first I had to identify what information the parents brought to the counseling session.

Parents, and other clients, are not empty vessels into which a therapist can ladle facts. Almost always there is already something in the container, some layman's theory about the origin of the problem. Often these theories are contradictory to established clinical concepts. This happened so frequently in our work that we formulated a clinical truism: *There is never an absence of information, there is misinformation.* It is difficult not to make some interpretation of events; the brain abhors an intellectual vacuum. Since the parents may be acting on their own interpretation of the cause and nature of stuttering, it is important for the therapist to get it out into the open.

During the initial interview, Mr. Brannon related this "theory" about the origin of Colin's speech disfluency. It was one we had not heard before, and we have heard many.

> Every summer we go to my folks' place. They live on a small farm north of here and raise a little bit of everything. Well, last year when Colin was just turned three, we were there visiting while my Dad had a bunch of suckling pigs. I was going to take them over to sell to a neighbor and put nine of the little porkers in a burlap sack and stuck it in the trunk of the car. Colin likes to go places with me; he follows me around all the time. Anyway, he sneaked into the back of the car and I didn't know he was there. Later, when I got in and started the car, the pigs all squealed at once, just set up a terrible racket. Colin didn't know the pigs were there and was so frightened he couldn't talk for three days. Seems like he stuttered from then on.

Resisting my impulse to make some joke about Porky Pig and "Th-th-that's all, folks," I praised the parents for bringing Colin in at just the right time. Many parents, I pointed out, employ some old misguided home remedies which actually make the problem worse. Together as a team, I reassured them, we can prevent Colin from growing up with the albatross of stuttering. Taken from a tape recording of the counseling session, this is exactly what I told Mr. and Mrs. Brannon about how stuttering develops:

> Let us suppose that every time you had an interruption in your speech, someone close to you reacted in some way. Whenever you paused, they would suggest that you should think about what you are trying to say, whenever you fumbled for a word they would tell you to relax, stop and start over again, or take a deep breath. How long would it take before you would become concerned about the way you talked and begin to doubt your ability in expressing yourself?
>
> This is essentially what happens to children beginning to stutter. Someone important to the child (a parent, any relative, a teacher, the child's companions) becomes concerned about the interruptions in his speech. Someone thinks that the child is beginning to stutter. When the normal speech interruptions are labeled as stuttering, the natural advice is to stop and start over, take a deep breath, think what you are

> going to say, slow down or, in desperation and anger, STOP STUTTERING. The child then becomes concerned about the interruptions in his speech; he begins to doubt his ability to talk. The child does not know what he is doing wrong but he will try hard to please his listeners. He will start to force, to put more effort and pressure into talking. Talking is not fun then! The child's struggles to prevent the interruptions will tend to make the adult listener think that his diagnosis of stuttering was correct. The adult will see the new forcings and efforts in the child's speech attempts and will exert more pressure on the child not to speak like that. This will lead to more effort and more broken speech by the child. The vicious cycle becomes more and more difficult to stop.

I held six additional counseling sessions with the Brannons during the fall semester. The meetings were devoted to designing ways to improve the parent-child communication. The best suggestions came from the parents themselves. Mrs. Brannon, for example, made this report at the fourth session:

> You know, I found out what a token listener I am with Colin . . . maybe with others, too. The other day I came home from a meeting and he followed me into the den trying to tell me something. I was still thinking about the meeting, opening my mail, and trying to catch fragments of the news on the radio. Colin started stuttering very badly and I realized I had been nodding and saying "ummmm" to him when he was trying to ask a question. I have to learn to be a better listener. So my husband and I talked it over and are starting a policy where the listener has to paraphrase what the speaker has said before he can reply.

At the end of the holiday season, the Brannons called me at home and reported that Colin was doing just fine. They felt no need to return to the clinic and wished me Happy New Year. This therapeutic encounter took place a long time ago and I watched with pleasure over the years as Colin earned accolades as a high school debater and later joined his father as a junior partner in a thriving financial planning business.

Working with adult stutterers was a challenge I undertook with great enthusiasm. The more severe the problem, the better I liked it. During my three-decade tenure in higher education, I helped many men find their way out of the thickets of halting speech. I also failed with some, and they linger uneasily on my mind even now.

The saga of one client, Richard, is characteristic of many others. A thirty-four-year-old tree trimmer, he came reluctantly to the clinic after a particularly frustrating experience. His wife, Karen, had just given birth to their first son after three episodes of false labor. Each time they had gone to the hospital, Richard had to answer a myriad of questions for the admitting clerks. Each time he had stuttered severely.

Richard was one of the most severe stutterers I have known. He had long audible blocks whereby he held onto the initial vowel in a prolonged groan. I timed one monster block at 17 seconds. In order to release the tension and escape from the block he used three bizarre strategies: he closed his eyes and stamped his foot (when he was really stuck he seemed to do a little St. Vitus Dance); he spit (either liquid or dry—at one time someone had told him to "spit it out"); worst of all, he swore. Persons who stutter are often totally fluent when using expletives. As the foreman of a tree service crew, he often had to contact homeowners to determine what they wanted done with their landscaping. One day I put on my old tree trimming clothes and went along with Richard on his appointed rounds. I was appalled. We stopped at a beautiful split-level house at 8:30 a.m. A middle-aged lady appeared at the door in a pink robe and then the show began. "You know, that doggone, that there," Richard gurgled, pointing at a large maple tree. "Damn it, I mean, oh, shit . . . " The longer he was stuck on a word, the more obscene he became. The lady was dumbfounded.

Later in the truck he told me about an even more embarrassing incident that happened when he married Karen. The minister officiating at the service knew Richard was a severe stutterer and, wanting to spare him, as well as the congregation, from long agonizing delays or blasphemy, suggested that instead of saying the vows aloud, Richard could *think* the words at the appropriate time. Many times later during the marriage, particularly when Richard and Karen had an argument, he would inform her, with a small smile, that well, maybe he was not really thinking "I do" when they got married. I liked Richard's sense of humor.

How to cope clinically with the chaos of his stuttering? The easiest way is to reduce the clinical task down to the two lowest common denominators: learn how to do the stuttering easily with a minimum of tension and hurry, and drain away all the negative emotion associated with stuttering and the act of communication.

After some minor resistance—which I and all of my clients have shown—Richard rapidly learned to shape the form of his disfluency so that it was simple and forward-moving. We worked before a mirror, duplicated the old hard stuttering and then compared it to an easier manner of utterance. Shifting back and forth, first in the safety of a clinic room and then in increasingly more complex settings, Richard came to see that he was his own worst enemy. He almost shouted "*Eureka!*" when he found he could be in charge of his own mouth.

The old negative memories of pain and frustration are reduced by a program of desensitization. We generally start from the easiest speaking situation and then gradually expand until we confront actual social encounters. Richard started up a hierarchy from easiest to most difficult and when he was about midway, he rebelled.

"Is this going to lead up to my most feared situation?" he asked. When I replied that it was, he said, "Let's go for broke, okay? Let's go out and confront my worst fear, because then I'll know I can do all the easier stuff." With some reluctance, I agreed. Richard's worst fear, the penultimate in his pantheon of stuttering trauma, was to encounter a "monster block," to be stuck on a word and not be able to finish.

It works best if the client devises his own assignments so I let Richard set up the speaking circumstance in which he was going to confront his worst fear. He decided to go to a local hardware and greenhouse and hold on to the initial sound "*sh*" until the clerk, not Richard, was overwhelmed. I should have known that his zany sense of humor would kick in.

Richard approached the counter of Heath's Hardware and Greenhouse, a huge rambling complex offering everything from animal feed to monkey wrenches for sale, and confronted a young male clerk.

"I want some sh . . . sh . . . sh . . . sh," he intoned in his prolonged way of stuttering. This was all purposeful and voluntary stuttering. The clerk's head snapped up and his eyes widened in surprise and concern.

"Sh-sh-sh," Richard persisted, relishing that he, not the listener, was in control of the situation. The clerk jerked out of his frozen posture and began bringing items: a box of shotgun shells, then a chamois cloth, then shoelaces, then another box of rifle ammunition. Richard kept intoning the "sh." Finally, in a moment of desperation, the clerk ran to the back of the store and returned with a large bag of sheep manure! Richard and I laughed so hard on the way back to town that I had to pull off the highway and surrender to the hilarity.

That single episode was a major breakthrough in Richard's struggle with the stuttering demons. By the end of the year he was talking almost as well as I and clearly he was enjoying his new found freedom. He served as a peer counselor for my other clients; he spoke at PTA meetings, service clubs and adult study groups about stuttering and how listeners should respond to persons with the problem. He laced his message with humor.

We became good friends. Therapists must be very careful about the nature of their relationship with clients. I always worried that the stutterer would become too dependent on me and that whatever improvement he made was an artifact of the relationship and not truly his own. But Richard was a mature person and we managed to do things together without damaging the treatment process. We both liked to gather wood for winter fireplace use, pick blueberries and jog on the many woodland paths around Marquette. Most of all, we enjoyed "humbugging."

We shared a mutual distaste for the commercialization of Christmas. Quite by accident, we created an entire new sport and art form. Starting in early October, we searched the dollar stores and the too-early holiday sales displays, purchased the most garish decorations we could find, and in the dark of the night put them up on each other's homes or vehicles. This continued, much to the amusement of our neighbors, until a final celebratory breakfast on National Humbug Day, December 21st.

Richard went on from that therapy year to teach in the public schools, and provide social work and then computer services for a state agency. He lived life zestfully until a dark night last winter on icy roads and an unavoidable auto accident which took his life. Some of the light went out of the lives of all who had known him, but the joy of being graced with his friendship remains.

Despite my commitment to help my fellow stutterers the way I had been helped, the client who may have affected me most profoundly was an adult with a language disorder. Experienced clinicians agree that therapy is a reciprocal encounter—the worker, too, grows or is otherwise changed by his relationship with a client.

Brenda Pendarvis, her friends and family agreed, was a remarkable woman: positive, energetic, compassionate and very independent. Following a stroke at the age of 49, she found herself dependent on others, unable to carry on a simple conversation, read a newspaper or even follow a recipe. During her treatment at our clinic, Mrs. Pendarvis touched the lives of scores of students with her charm, loving character and abiding good will. My twenty-year association with her all started with her daughter.

When Sarah Pendarvis, a sophomore speech therapy student in one of my classes, described her mother's stroke and slow recovery from aphasia, the possibility of offering therapy seemed very remote. Mrs. Pendarvis lived with her family in a small village in the Keweenaw Peninsula, an isolated region of Michigan's Upper Peninsula where copper was discovered more than 150 years ago. Yet the more Sarah talked about her mother's condition, particularly the gains she had made with treatment limited to two weekly visits by a public school speech clinician, the more I wanted to meet Mrs. Pendarvis to determine her potential for more intensive rehabilitation. Later that autumn, when I was scheduled to visit the Copper Country to consult with several speech clinicians at a local intermediate school district, I invited Sarah to come along on the trip. Following my meeting with the clinicians, we drove to Calumet to visit Mrs. Pendarvis.

Brenda Pendarvis is the type of person who radiates warmth, openness, sincerity. In fact, after she greeted her daughter with an affectionate hug, impulsively I, too, embraced her. Eagerly, she tried to describe for me the impact her illness had upon her life and how much she wanted to regain her former level of functioning. In earlier discussions, Sarah had outlined the precipitous onset of her mother's illness as far as she could recall. But only Brenda could relate what the experience had been like and now, at our initial meeting, she attempted to piece together her fragmented memories. Much later, after she had recovered her communication skills more completely, Mrs. Pendarvis assembled her recollections in a comprehensive diary of her illness. Here is how she described the stroke:

> I was at home in Calumet in the Copper Country of Michigan's Upper Peninsula. It was Tuesday, January 11, 1974. I woke up at 7:00 a.m. to a terrible blizzard. Learning that school was canceled for the day, I made a big kettle of soup and let it simmer. Then I woke my two youngest children, Sarah and Scott. I gave them a nice breakfast and, feeling tired and headachy—which was unusual for me—went upstairs to stretch out on the bed for a few minutes of rest. My neck felt stiff. I must have passed out because when I tried to get up, I couldn't move. My whole right side was paralyzed, numb; I couldn't scream or call out. I knew that there was something terribly wrong with me. In a short while—I'm not certain how long I lay there—Sarah called upstairs to ask me where the cookie recipes were. When I did not answer, she came up and looked at me. My face was crooked and my right eye was drawn down. She turned and ran for help.

Mrs. Pendarvis had come a long way in the two years since she suffered the stroke. She had experienced limited spontaneous recovery from the initially severe physical and language impairments. No longer paralyzed, she could now care for herself, talk coherently, though slowly and with considerable word searching. With some assistance in deciphering recipes, she had resumed preparing meals for her family. The initial stages of recovery, however, had been very difficult. Here is another excerpt from her retrospective account of her illness:

> My speech and my actions were all mixed up. When I started to say something, the words would not come out and I became upset. All I could say was "Shit!" And I had always detested that word. Now I know that many people with the same problem were the same way. There were many strange things I would say, like, "I died," as if I had come back to life. As I sat at the dinner table, my family would hand me food and encourage me to name the items, but I called everything "catsup" or "fish." I thought I was talking normally. I even had difficulty remembering my children's names. I would look at Sarah and say "Scott." Everything was so confusing. I would get things backward, like "up" for "down," "here" for "there" and "he" for "she." One thing that helped me most was when Sarah put labels on furniture all over the house. And she would sit patiently with me in the kitchen and help me understand a recipe.

Despite her achievements, though, Mrs. Pendarvis was acutely aware of the distance yet to go if she hoped to regain even a semblance of her prior abilities. I sensed, by nonverbal cues and what she did not share in that initial encounter, that her days were filled with quiet desperation and that she was hanging onto her present life by a slim margin. One final entry from her diary confirmed my intuition:

> I wasn't able to talk well at all and I got very depressed. Sometimes I would wonder, "God, why am I doing these things?" I would place things on the dining room table that I wanted to leave for the children, in little

> piles, this for Sarah, this for Scott. Then I would take a whole handful of pills and think that if I swallowed all of them, I would pass away. And I wanted to! But then I would picture my family and everyone else who were so kind to me and I would put the pills away. Thoughts of suicide returned to me many times during my convalescence. I cried a lot.

We devised an intensive therapy program for Mrs. Pendarvis consisting of four phases: 1) daily contact (9:00 a.m. to 4:00 p.m.) with evening stimulation-recreation for a five-week interval while she is in temporary residence at the university; 2) weekly contact (one and one-half days per week) at the clinic; she will commute for these sessions; 3) bimonthly follow-up sessions in her own residence; and 4) intermittent follow-up, either at the university or in her home setting.

There are several distinct treatment approaches to select from when planning a therapy program for an adult aphasic. The type of therapy I intended to use with Mrs. Pendarvis consisted of multidimensional language stimulation: I wanted her to reach out for language as a natural extension of ideas and concepts drawn from her past. I would seek to re-energize old associations to work again rather than create new ones. In addition, I planned to do specific work on vocabulary building, increase in retention span, and improvement of reading and writing skills. Every effort would be made to keep the activities and materials relevant to the client's interests and life situation.

As I prepared to do trial therapy with Brenda, I remembered her interest in cooking, her desire to decipher recipes and her Cornish heritage. Cornwall is a small duchy located on the far southwest coast of England. The Cornish are noted for expertise in mining, fine singing, and distinctive foods, most notably, the pasty, a distinctive meat pie. Combining all three of Brenda's interests, I selected an old recipe for a particular type of dessert indigenous to Cornwall and brought to the Copper Country by immigrant miners in the late nineteenth century. Here is a transcript of a portion of the trial therapy session showing how the food item was used:

Clinician: Food from Cornwall is the topic for our session.

Brenda: Oh, really . . . !

Clinician: Yes. Here is a small piece of a type of pastry.

Brenda: I know, I know . . . that's ahh . . . oh, my mother used to make it all the time.

Clinician: Can you think of the name for it?

Brenda: (ten second pause)

Clinician: It starts with "h."

Brenda: Heavy cake!

Clinician: Right!

Brenda: But, ah, there was . . . different name for it. Heavy . . . heavy . . . duff. I haven't thought of that for years.

Clinician: Heavy duff is right; it's made . . .

Brenda: It has raisins . . . ah, what did the old folks, they used, small raisins, ah, currants.

Space limitations do not permit inclusion of the complete transcript; this is a list of the activities that comprised the remainder of the trial therapy session:

The ingredients of the pastry were enumerated and each item was described and cataloged.

The items were then used for retention span drill.

The client wrote or copied the name of each ingredient.

The proportion of each ingredient used in the pastry was studied. Since Brenda had considerable difficulty comprehending numbers, a pictorial system was devised (the direction "3 cups of flour" was depicted graphically as three full measuring cups beside the word "flour.")

The final activity proved to be the most stimulating to Mrs. Pendarvis: we began a list of other Cornish delicacies.

Mrs. Pendarvis was reluctant to leave the therapy room when the session ended. Prior to her stroke, she said she had begun to trace her family roots in the Copper Country—would we help her now as part of her speech therapy program? When a client suggests her own theme for therapy, particularly a topic that combined numbers and dates, reading, writing and interviewing source persons, a clinician realizes that his labors will be refreshingly easy.

At the end of the five-week intensive therapy program, Brenda Pendarvis had improved dramatically. She radiated confidence in herself. She resumed using the telephone, clipped and studied advertisements in the local newspaper, began to shop for the family groceries without assistance, and started the immense job of sorting and filing her large collection of ethnic recipes. She even acquired a pamphlet of traffic rules and began preparing to reacquire her driver's license, which had lapsed during her recovery from the stroke.

At the onset of the follow-up period, we added two new facets to Brenda's treatment program. In order to increase her level of activity and provide for greater social contact with a variety of people, I encouraged her to work as a volunteer receptionist in a local nursing home. I also arranged for her to visit with several adult aphasics living in her home region. Mrs. Pendarvis enjoyed the activities immensely and the people she contacted looked forward to her visits.

The second addition to her therapy program was a fortuitous choice. I asked Brenda to keep a daily diary in which she was to record, as best she could, her thoughts, feelings and observations. The primary purpose of the diary was to facilitate improvement in her writing skills. Keeping a daily diary prompted Mrs. Pendarvis to a new and encompassing challenge: to tell her own story of the brain injury, convalescence and eventual recovery. It took more than a year to edit the entries in her diary, interview various relatives and piece together the fragments of her recollections. Several times she almost abandoned the task in frustration, but finally the booklet, which she titled *Comeback after a Stroke*, was completed. When the booklet was published and she held it in her hands for the first time, Mrs. Pendarvis looked fondly at the members of her treatment team who had assembled for a reception in her honor and said, "You have given me back my life." There was not a dry eye in the room.

At the present time, we see Brenda Pendarvis only on an intermittent basis, and then only for short social visits. Except for some residual difficulty with arithmetic, she is functioning as a normal individual. One final excerpt from her diary reveals how her life has taken on new meaning:

> I remember the feeling of being a "mummy" when I could barely speak. In spite of all the troubles of the past, I am happy that I'm capable of doing so many things now. I'm learning more every day and continually strive to improve my reading and writing. Above all, my numbers are coming back to me. A person has to be happy in their heart and soul. To relax and forget the past. There is always tomorrow. We get too impatient. To me, that is the secret of it all. I can live gracefully as an aphasic. Lately, I have been very busy and I have accomplished many things.
>
> Right now I am happy and content. It has been 5 years since my stroke and in the last 3 weeks, I feel it has all been worth it. I shall be a more graceful, middle-aged woman from now on.

The most important role of a speech therapist is to activate the healing resources of the client. We accomplish this by the very essence of our being, a timeless total immersion in a task in which we both lose and find ourselves.

I always thanked my clients for the opportunity to share their struggle for growth. When doing therapy, we are not so much selfless as we become our best selves. We are ennobled by service to others and it gives us a purpose well beyond our own limited life.

Maxim #6 ***Strive to be a "There you are" rather than a "Here I am" kind of listener.***

We swim daily in an ocean of words. Despite the fact that we have two ears and consequently should listen twice as much as we talk, good listeners are an endangered species.

The "Here I am" persons hear but don't really listen. They are simply waiting for their turn to talk if they wait at all. Although two individuals seem to be in conversation, "Here I am" persons are really carrying on a serial monologue. Sometimes the dissonance is very obvious.

As I was preparing to write this chapter, I happened to visit a country store where I know the proprietor well. Dave had recently suffered a broken leg and his recovery was progressing slowly. When I asked how the rehabilitation was going, Dave started to share his experience. Another customer interrupted and began to talk about his own fracture the previous year. Violating the social norms–the lousy listening was so bad I couldn't help myself–I stopped the customer bluntly by asking, "I thought this was about Dave?"

The "There you are" persons are good listeners. They really attend to and respond to what others are saying. They are seen as empathic, caring people and are sought out by others. When people are listened to, when they are allowed to tell their story without interruptions or references to ourselves, you can almost see them grow and expand.

Why are empathic listeners the few, the prized, the marveled? My view is that we all have somewhere deep in our psyche the illusion that we are the center of events; we tend to reference everything we experience in terms of ourselves. This might be termed the principle of "immaculate perception," the core belief that the way we see things is the right, the normal, the good way. While paying lipservice to acknowledging all viewpoints, we harbor the notion that if other people would only get with the program, they would look at circumstances through our perfect lense and they would agree with us. The following anonymous short verse sums it up:

"In matters controversial,
My perception's rather fine.
I appreciate all points of view
Those that are wrong and mine."

LET THE CRAZINESS EMERGE

The chairman of the library committee droned on and on about the need to prioritize—the then current buzz word—all requests to supplement institutional holdings. Shuffling through a thick folder, he paused occasionally to cite some administrative memorandum. I looked longingly out the window at the late afternoon sun slanting through the pines. "How much longer can this go on?" I thought desperately. I had clients to see, students to counsel and my family waiting at home to go on a spring picnic.

Eager to be a part of the academic governance, I accepted requests to serve on various committees—the faculty senate, awards committee, the library committee and, because I wanted to see what happens there, the committee-on-committees. Answer: not much. "Minutes are kept and hours are wasted," an elderly professor told me one day in the Faculty lounge. At first I thought he was simply cynical after all his years of service, but I soon found out that committee business moves at a glacial pace. And it seemed to be a forum for some politically inclined professors to parade and posture. The prickly edges of large egos lurked just beneath the surface of the seemingly collegial discussions. For a clearer idea of how faculty committees work, imagine an academic theme park run by Curly, Larry and Moe.

What could I do to escape the tedium and self-conscious solemnity of committee service? Finally my zany sense of humor came to the rescue.

At the next meeting, I kept silent all the while the committee members were debating some thorny academic issue. Finally, just as the group was growing weary and a vote appeared imminent, I interrupted the proceedings.

Since I had not said a word, they had to listen to me.

"How did that fly get on the ceiling?" I asked with great seriousness. "Did it crawl up the wall? Or did it buzz aloft and then suddenly turn over to land?"

The committee members looked at each other in bemusement, if not alarm, and my reputation was established: Emerick does not work well on committees. I smiled all the way back to the speech clinic. In my last few years at the university, some eager young instructors asked: "How did you find the time to write all those articles and books?" At the time, I just made some vague remarks about time allocation, but now I can share my secret with all those bored masses yearning to be free of committee ennui.

Free of committee assignments, I set about fulfilling what now seems like a puerile ambition for my academic career: In the first decade I would do everything, go anywhere; the second decade would be devoted to writing about what I had discovered during the first ten years; the third decade would be given over to my dotage, a time to be the forgetful but loveable old professor.

There was a real opportunity to be a pioneer in those early days. I traipsed all over the Upper Peninsula talking with school administrators about the need for remedial speech, met with and offered assistance to speech therapists working in area schools, gave workshops from Ironwood to Sault Ste. Marie. Neither did I turn down any offers to give lectures and workshops across the country. From Tampa to Duluth, from Washington, D.C. to Chicago, I shared my expertise and experiences with any group that would pay the airfare. Finally one night I found myself in Chicago O'Hare airport waiting for a delayed flight to Pittsburgh, in the company of scores of weary businessmen with sore feet and enlarged prostates. It was then that I asked the most profound of existential questions: "Why am I doing this?" I had a loving young family, wonderful students and a gorgeous environment in which to live. It was time to go home and write those books before my bunions and prostate got the better of me.

When I asked the head librarian where I might find some quiet space in which to start writing my first book, she fixed me with a disapproving stare over her half-glasses.

"This is a teaching college," she hissed, and turned back to the card catalog.

My response was to arise an hour earlier each morning and tap out a book about stuttering on an old portable typewriter. Texts about diagnosis in speech therapy and audiometry followed. But I always maintained perspective: I was a teacher who happened to write, not a writer who sometimes taught.

More books and scholarly articles followed. As I gained some recognition in the field of speech therapy, I was astonished at how my university colleagues reacted to my literary success. I think I expected at least some approval, maybe even a bit of professional recognition from my colleagues. But there were no accolades. Most ignored the achievements. Some professors on the speech therapy staff went to great lengths to find suitable substitutes to my book for use as an assigned text in their classes. After presenting the department head with a complimentary copy of a legendary introductory text in our field, which I had been selected to coauthor for its 8th edition, I was called into his office so that he could point out a typographical error on page 327. Thank you very much.

Some few colleagues were openly angry at my publishing accomplishments. One professor, a longtime fixture at the university, stopped me in the library one day and launched into a diatribe.

"Who do you think you are, young man?" he asked rhetorically through clenched teeth. "What makes you think that your views are worthy of print?" I sputtered something in response but he cut me off with a dismissive gesture. "It's just a textbook, anyway, hardly that creative," he spat. As he turned to walk away, I remembered something Schopenhauer wrote and I quoted it to his retreating figure:

"Works like this are as a mirror: if an ass looks in you cannot expect an angel to look out."

When I related that experience to my friend, John Argeropoulos, university counselor and fellow author, he smiled ruefully. Despite his publications and myriad of invitations to conduct workshops on stress management, his own department head and a committee of peers temporized for several years on a well-deserved promotion in academic rank. We were sitting beside a waterfall admiring the magic of flowing water and I regretted that I had brought up a negative issue in such a beautiful spot.

"No, it's ok," John began. "I think many faculty members promised themselves that someday they would accomplish a significant scholarly project. Time goes by and they think about it at odd moments but there is always the press of other duties. Now, you did it. You fulfilled the dream and, for them, it is a vivid reminder of their inability to realize an elusive fantasy."

We sat for a while admiring a winter wren's tinkling sonata. John sighed in satisfaction and said finally, "Everybody has an opinion."

The wren was offering a reprise when I had a sudden insight. "I'm having a professorial hot flash," I blurted out. "An aphorism is being born: *All opinions are not created equal.*"

Familiar with my wild flights of Celtic excess, John asked, "How so?"

"Well, while everyone has a *right* to his or her opinion, they can confuse that right with the assumption that all opinions are of equal value," I responded.

"Sure," John said, after a thoughtful pause. "An informed or educated opinion is better than one from a neophyte. I may have an opinion about the cause of stuttering, but I wouldn't put it in the same league with yours."

At any rate, the university administrators were ecstatic about my books and scholarly papers. When a new text was published, the provost gave autographed copies to each member of the university board of control. In short order I was promoted to full professor, received a distinguished faculty award and was granted a sabbatical leave.

However, my old tendency to poke holes in the balloons of pomposity through the use of humor sometimes put me out of favor on the top floor of the administration building. The provost invited five faculty members who had made significant scholarly contributions to attend a luncheon with the university's controlling board. It turned out that the provost had orchestrated an elaborate "show and tell" time to persuade the Board that, as dean of the faculty, he was responsible in no small measure for our achievements. Almost as if we were grade school children, the provost went down the row of invited faculty asking each of us to talk about our current scholarly projects. I was fourth in line. The provost went on at some length in his introduction, listing and describing the books I had published and how he had been told by his fellow deans in other universities how fortunate he was to have Dr. Emerick on *his* faculty. Then he made a mistake. Turning to me, he suggested, "Why don't you tell the Board what you are writing now, Dr. Emerick?"

The members of the Board turned their collective gray eminences toward me expectantly. There was a long tense pause while I struggled with my jester demon. I could not contain myself.

"Well, this morning, I wrote a long letter to my mother," I finally said, using my best Jimmy Stewart "aw-shucks" impression.

I thought it was funny at the time. Still do. And at least one member of the board did, too, because I saw the broad smile she tried to hide behind a cinnamon roll. It was worth the mild rebuke I got from my department head later in the day.

In those early days, trained as a scientist, I interpreted any coincidence as simply random happenstance. Now I have put away such childish thoughts and learned to pay attention to cosmic synchronicity. . . more about that later. Fortunately, just when I needed help, Russell Davis joined the faculty in the speech therapy department. This was the very same Russ who, many years before, astonished the hospital nurses by lifting me aloft in a celebratory wrestling hold when our twin daughters were born. He swept into our lives again with an invigorating swirl of energy and enthusiasm just as we were sagging under the heavy load of a major curriculum revision. (The inmates of academe get restless every few years and siphon off the excess energy by tinkering with the building blocks. It makes them feel that they are progressing. Usually they change things back to the original state in the next episode of disquiet.) Along with the revision of most courses, we had a new bevy of graduate students and preparation of state and federal grants to sustain the growth of the department.

For me personally, Russ helped to reinvigorate my devotion to nature and outdoor adventures. While I did not realize it and would have dismissed any attempt to alter my approach to work, my life was out of balance. It's difficult in the rush of daily events to recognize you have become a workaholic.

Maxim #7 ***Let the craziness emerge at least once a day.***

Mirth is good for the soul and the body, and adults need to do more of it. It matters not if others are not amused by our antics and admonish us to grow up.

A philosopher pointed out that solemnity is a disease. At least once each day–more often would be better–allow yourself to do something silly. If you have forgotten how to be playful, invite some kids to share your day. They know. If you make humor and laughter life companions, you will always have sunshine in your soul.

I expect the reader is aware by now that I have a crazy temperament and that a higher than average number of peculiar events happen to me. Perhaps it's the result of some quirky cosmic design. My response to many situations is to find something funny, some silly incongruity, to lighten the seriousness. This trait, the ability to put people at ease with humor, I consider an asset. It also can be a great liability. (I believe that any asset can be, and often is, a liability if relied on too much). One example from my many academic misadventures:

> The university had been trying to lure a distinguished scholar away from another institution. Since the professor had a son enrolled at Northern, the university administrators decided to invite Dr. C. Leeland Graham for a weekend visit during the autumnal color season. When it was learned that the famous professor was an avid hunter, the Dean requested that I invite him to my favorite woodland spots.
>
> Dean Carpenter can't be blamed for what happened. How was he to know of my propensity for getting lost, or even worse, a familial trait of uncontrolled laughing when some untoward event occurs?
>
> Early one October morning I dropped the portly professor and his son beside a river, drew a crude map in the sand and

admonished them to meet me upstream at a log bridge in two hours. I was sending them into my favorite grouse coverts.

When they did not show up at the appointed time, I blew my whistle, shouted, and began to get mildly concerned. As I drove up and down woods roads honking the car horn, I began to imagine the headlines in our local newspaper: ***Famous professor lost in woods***. I began to get the nervous giggles about the impossible situation I was in.

It was almost dark when the pair emerged wraith-like from a swampy area–tired, thirsty, hungry, spattered with mud and whipped with alder branches. It still would have ended all right if I could have stifled the long-repressed laughter, but I burst forth in loud guffaws and rolled helplessly in the ferns.

We never heard from the august academician again but there was some furtive inquiry into the tenure rules of the university to see if I was safe from understandable outrage.

I sent a note to Dean Carpenter, a biblical scholar, and included this verse from Proverbs 17:22: "A merry heart doeth good like a medicine; but a broken spirit drieth the bones."

Dean Carpenter sent a note back to me with only this quote: "We suffer as much from our virtues as our vices." By his initials he had drawn a smiley face.

RESTORING BALANCE

There it was parked in the driveway: a sleek new green pickup truck and, on its back, a state-of-the-art molded plastic camper. Sure, I had agreed with Lynn that we needed to get out and learn more about the beautiful Upper Peninsula. But it was now a metal, glass and plastic reality. It was a gorgeous rig and I should be eager to explore a new spring season. What had I done? How could I leave my clients, the students depending on me, my burgeoning literary success?

True, it was May, the semester was over, and I had reluctantly decided to take a long break from my duties, the first extended vacation from the academic world in almost two decades. My work role at the university would not resume until late August. Shouldn't I have been ecstatic?

Why was I so ambivalent? I knew my life was out of balance, realized it more fully two weeks before when I found myself outlining a therapy plan during an intermission at a university theater production. Work was dominating my life—but that's what men in our culture do, right? My wise and wonderful Life Partner knew that I just needed a wee push.

"When you're teetering on the edge of a precipice," she observed quietly, "the only prudent thing to do is take a step backward." She was right, of course. I have always had great difficulty negotiating the emotional topography of change. I realized that I must go back, as I had done long ago as a troubled young stutterer, to the solace of nature.

Have you ever skipped through a forest decorated in new green foliage with a four-year-old child? Now, multiply that image by two. Lynn and Mary frolicked about like colts let out to spring pasture. They admired newly bloomed trillium and Dutchman's breeches wildflowers, paused to say hello to a sleepy toad just emerged from a long winter's nap, and splashed happily in a small stream. We were on our way to pay our respects to Laughing Whitefish Falls.

The towering waterfall was surging over the sandstone ledges in the full voice of spring. We watched in awe as the river bounced and danced over the rocks; Mary placed her hand in mine and said softly, "Daddy, it's singing to me." Squeezing her hand gently, I glanced over at her twin sister, Lynn—whose name in Gaelic means "waterfall." Her eyes were shining as if reflecting the sparkle of the water.

What a magical time we had, roaming around the far reaches of our native valley in the green camper truck. Those shared outdoor experiences not only corrected the imbalance in my life, it also brought our family closer together. We didn't know it then, but the seeds planted during those adventures would grow and blossom many years later: in the girls' choice of careers in the out-of-doors, in a volume portraying the splendors of the Upper Peninsula, and in a renewed dedication to help preserve this wondrous land in its pristine state.

And you know, God didn't even notice—much less care—that I was not laboring in the speech clinic. My nose was briefly out of joint with typical workaholic hubris to learn that the university was running smoothly without me, thank you very much.

Two years later, when I was awarded a sabbatical to write a book, I experienced very little separation anxiety over abandoning my professorial role. I'm not sure the powers that administer universities fully comprehend how a sabbatical transforms university teachers. Time and again I have seen colleagues at Northern and other universities changed forever by the experience of a year to study, write and travel. There is sensuous joy in lingering over an idea or savoring the comfort of an extended margin of time unfurling ahead. A sabbatical means surcease from a myriad of urgent tugs on your synapses. You have the opportunity to deal with the important, not just rush to accomplish the urgent. The relief descends like a benediction. During my extended leaves, I concurred again and again with the couplet from William Davies' poem, *Leisure*

> "A poor life this, if full of care
> we have no time to stand and stare."

Energized by the leisure of a wide margin in my life, I completed the book at the midpoint of the sabbatical year. We took the children out of school, packed our gear and headed west in our camper truck. Tom Sawyer's whitewashed fence, Mesa Verde, the Grand Canyon, Olympic National Park, Custer State Park—places where our ranger daughters would later work—we visited them all. So this is how the other half lives, I thought. I didn't once think about speech therapy.

Well, that's not strictly true. On the Little Bighorn Battlefield in eastern Montana, another visitor asked me if I knew where to find the grave markers for the Gray Horse Troop—and he was a stutterer! He took umbrage at my broad grin until I explained why I found the circumstances amusing.

It certainly was not amusing when, during a routine physical exam several years after our return, Dr. Wilson informed me that my blood pressure was too high. I was given a prescription and the usual admonition about monitoring my life style. Suddenly, the specter of familial hypertension appeared. My grandfather, father and older brother all suffered with high blood pressure. In each instance, the disease was first detected in early middle age; they were forced to lead a limited life style and finally became totally dependent on medication. Remembering the myriad of side effects my older relatives endured with their medication, I threw away the prescription and took off running for my life.

At first, I ran for health. Within a month, I noticed that my stamina had increased dramatically, that I was less susceptible to stress, and my blood pressure was coming down. Anyone who runs seriously knows that he usually alters many other aspects of his life to keep pace with the benefits of vigorous exercise: I stopped smoking my beloved pipe, watched my diet carefully and learned to pace myself better on the job. At present, I run for both my health and for mental repose. I have become addicted to the jogger's high; oiled by the body's easy rhythms, my mind springs free and soars in the tree tops.

A long hard run through the forest is an excellent transition from work to home—all the tensions, frustrations and uncertainties built up during the day are sloughed off as my body labors as it was intended to do. Each stride is a celebration of life.

Soon my daughters, now teenagers, were attracted by my passion for running. We developed a common interest that maintained parent-child connections during those intense and difficult years of transition from a child to adulthood. When their mother joined us for our daily ritual, we became a family on the run. After daughter Lynn made the university cross-country team, she introduced me to competitive running. Almost immediately, I was hooked on racing.

When I entered my first 5K race, I was uncertain about how to proceed. While I was fit from all the running I had done, I had never competed before and was not sure what to expect. I picked out a man who seemed to be about my age and confessed I was a nervous beginner.

"Not to worry," he said reassuringly. "Here's what to do—look around, find the most curvaceous gal, and then follow her. That will take your mind off the race."

It worked wonderfully. I attached myself to a trim woman in pink shorts. The view was rewarding and the miles zipped by. I was surprised when I was across the finish line, winning third place in my age category and was awarded my very first medal. Later, during the post race camaraderie, I sought out my helpful advisor and told him in detail how his advice had made the race effortless.

"You should have seen her," I enthused. "She had on these tight fitting pink shorts!"

He looked at me in open-mouthed surprise, exhaled vigorously and, narrowing his eyes into malevolent slits, he exploded, "That was my wife, you dirty old man!"

For the better part of a decade, Lynn and I followed the summer road racing circuit all over the Upper Peninsula. I had never been much of an athlete but I found I could win, place or show in my age group at almost every race. I delighted in starting slowly and then passing entrants as I picked up speed. Yielding to humor again, one of my favorite tricks was to pull up next to a much younger contender and ask innocently, "Are you over fifty?"

Entering races put us in touch with many interesting people and I looked forward to seeing them at each new event. Nothing bonds individuals so quickly as sharing anaerobic misery and the agony of the feet. One autumn, as I ran in the eight-mile Mackinac Island Road Race, I glanced ahead and admired the undulating wave of bright colors worn by hundreds of runners rounding a curve beside Lake Huron; looking back I could see a similar chromatic parade. What a marvelous experience to be a part of that group activity, how comforting to feel (with John Muir) at that moment completely *in* and not just *on* the world.

Wherever we went on our outdoor adventures, we took along running shoes and shorts. We had many funny encounters. My all-time favorite racing experience took place in Northern Arizona at 7,000 foot altitude. My wife and I entered the Sacred Mountain Race sponsored by local Native Americans; we were the only Anglos at the starting line. Just before the starting gun went off, a yellow school bus pulled in and disgorged 43 Hopi children from Third Mesa. Lynn and I found ourselves running among the youngsters as they larked about us, chatting with each other and offering encouragement to us oxygen-starved whites. I went into a choking-laughing spasm when one Hopi lad, doing a good imitation of John Wayne, asked, "Does the name Custer mean anything to you folks?"

Running endowed me with health, happy involvement, good friends and a link to my daughters; it is a gift that continues to follow me all the days of my life.

Our lives were also immensely enriched when, after much searching, we found a gorgeous spot on Lake Superior to build a cabin. Lynn and I wore out several salesmen looking for just the right location for a remote redoubt.

"What do you want, exactly?" one real estate agent asked plaintively after yet another unsuccessful showing.

"We'll know it when we see it," we responded.

Finally, prompted by a small advertisement in the local paper, we discovered our personal "listening point" near Au Train. Since there was no road to the property, we had to compass our way to the site a mile or so through swampy terrain. One of our daughters even lost a shoe in the bog.

"If we buy this place, will we have to walk in through the swamp every time?" she asked, with remarkable equanimity.

When we reached the shoreline, we were all bug-bitten and branch-whipped. We stepped out onto large sandstone shelves and saw the immense blue of Lake Superior. Lynn and I looked at each other and said, "This is it!" at the same time.

By the end of the next summer, a road was built and our cedar log cabin stood in a small clearing by the shore. We call it the Au Train Hermitage; here our spirits have been enriched (with Keats) in the simple worship of many days.

It was at the Hermitage that we made the acquaintance of a family from Ohio who shared our affection for the land. Bob and Maggie Watson purchased some of the spectacular sandstone shoreline and woodland.

Since they already owned a beautifully crafted summer home on Perch Lake south of Munising in the Hiawatha National Forest, they had no immediate interest in building near Lake Superior. They simply loved the Big Lake and the opportunity to bring their family to explore, picnic and swim.

Our friendship was immediate. The Watsons had three sons, David, John and Tim. All three were runners. The middle son, John, was a gifted long-distance runner and he and I shared a special bond. Together, our two families devised an annual relay marathon: Each summer, all nine of us would carry a baton and a small vial of water between Lake Superior and Perch Lake. We ran the 28-mile course in segments of one, two or three miles and each participant chose where and how much he or she wished to run. Our marathon took us through heavily forested terrain on old woods roads. The summer running event continued for several years until, tragically, John was killed in a bizarre accident in Boston. Although the happy, fun-filled memories of the Perch Lake Superior Marathon remain with all of us, no one had the heart to continue the family tradition without John.

My heart was not in my work, either, at least not as completely as it had always been. I spent many days musing about my adolescent dream of being a literary naturalist.

In the Navajo tradition, when a tribal member becomes ill, the assumption is that the person's life is out of harmony with nature. The remedy consists of a secret ceremony designed to usher the sick individual back into synchrony with the healing powers of the earth. In my own quest for restoring balance, I relearned, not in the abstract but in my very synapses, what Thoreau meant when he said that he needed a "wide margin in his life." I thought back to the sabbatical year when that margin had changed my outlook and refocused my priorities. Now, as I struggled to maintain some harmony in my days, I began to feel the irresistible pull of the path not taken. I was being drawn back to my passion for the natural world. Perhaps I was ready for the next chapter in my life.

Maxim #8 ***Restoring Balance: Keep separate what you do for a living from who you are as a person.***

Avoid building your entire life around one thing. During my long tenure as a university professor of speech therapy, I always took exception when someone referred to me as a speech therapist or worse, "the professor." That was my profession, not my identity. Why am I making this distinction? If we put all of our self-esteem into the work role basket, when things don't go well on the job, as sometimes they do not, the impact can be devastating.

Fortunately, the clients we serve sometimes have a way of deflating our exalted sense of self-importance.

> One of our Master's students, Chad Benteen, went to Moorhead State College on my recommendation to work in a summer treatment program. It was his first job and Chad approached his labors with the same zeal and devotion he had witnessed during his training.
>
> A longtime resident of the Detroit area, Chad had very little understanding of the idiosyncracies of the mostly Scandinavian community in the western Minnesota region.
>
> One of his clients was an eight year old boy with a stuttering problem. Chad eagerly commenced a program of therapy which I had devised, a form of treatment which had worked well with many children.
>
> The child's grandmother brought the boy in for the 50-minute sessions four times a week and waited while Chad worked with him. At the end of each session, the grandmother asked, "Is that it, then?" And Chad responded with, "No, I'll see him tomorrow." The grandmother then looked out the window and

said, "Uff-dah," which Chad took to be a quirky Norwegian expression for "Thank you." This same verbal ritual continued throughout the six week summer session.

Before returning home, Chad decided to take in a local county fair. As he walked about inspecting the various exhibits, he noticed people wearing blue and white buttons inscribed with the expression "Uff-dah!". Finally, while waiting at a refreshment counter, he asked a young lady why she was wearing a button that said, "Thank you". The girl went into a prolonged laughing fit before gurgling that "Uff-dah" is the Scandinavian equivalent of the exasperated expression, "Oh, shit!"

Facts and attitude

The decision must have been the right one: As I walked down the hallway to the speech clinic mailboxes with my letter of resignation, I was whistling. The secretary looked up from her desk in surprise at the lilting Simon and Garfunkel melody *Feelin' Groovy*.

"Everything okay?" she asked a bit querulously.

"You'd better believe it, Pilgrim," I responded brightly, striking a John Wayne pose.

For several weeks I had agonized over the decision. When the university announced a generous buy out plan to encourage the "higher-paid" longtime professors to retire, I knew the time would never be any better. It was time to tell the department head what the raven told Poe.

The decade of the 1980s was not a pleasant time in our department. We faced declining enrollment, federal grants were drying up and there was endless anguish over the state of the budget. At almost every faculty meeting, the department head initiated the proceedings with the same jeremiad: "We are in jeopardy, double jeopardy," he would lament, "and if you have other options, you'd better think seriously about them." The rest of the meeting was spent convincing ourselves that we didn't have the funds to do anything.

Whereas I had always been eager to get to school, often arriving very early in the morning, I now found myself dawdling on the drive across town. More often than not I took the long way and cruised slowly along the shoreline of Lake Superior. When the wind was blowing stiffly, I parked and watched the sight of waves gruffing the shore for ten minutes or more, to get their glad tidings deep into my psyche. Even with those meditative respites, I still found that my toes were curled tightly in my shoes when I pulled into the parking lot.

Just when we thought our plates were overflowing with travail, a newly hired university president set out to break the bargaining power of the faculty union. The diminutive C.E.O. believed, wrongly it turned out, that he and his hired-gun-consultant could simply roll right over the bucolic faculty at the remote university. The leadership of the American Association of University Professors thought the president was attempting to demonstrate his prowess as an administrator, attract national attention, and then move on to a larger institution in a few years. The divisiveness and rancor were monumental.

Digging in for the long haul, the faculty voted to withhold services—a strike by any name—if the president did not back down from his opposition to the new contract. Only three suck-up troglodytes among more than 300 professors voted against the strike. A demonstration picket march was carried out one morning within view of the president's top-floor office in the administration building. The campus took on the atmosphere of a war zone. Even when the president capitulated on the contract, the resentment and adversarial climate continued.

My comrade Russ Davis, the only one on the speech therapy staff who shared my interests in hunting and outdoor rambles, devised elaborate schemes with me to escape the negative climate at the university. Even more wild and crazy than me, Russ could always be counted upon to take a soiree in the woods. He loved to explore the hinterlands but flatly refused to backtrack when we came to the end of some remote road. On one early September day, an old logging road we were following ended suddenly at the Escanaba River. Russ thought he could see where large logging trucks had forded the 100-yard wide, fast-flowing river. I was astounded when, with a shout of glee, he nosed his elderly 1965 Rambler into the swift current and headed for the opposite bank. At midstream, water seeped in through the cracks under my passenger-side door; at times we seemed to be floating downstream. When the car climbed the rocky bank on the far side, I began to laugh hysterically in relief. Then, noticing my camera on the seat, I impulsively asked Russ to back down into the river so I could commemorate the event. He still insists that I put him up to the stunt and rolls his eyes in mock exasperation when he retells the camera episode.

Back at the university, what disturbed me most was the passive attitude of so many students enrolled in my classes. They seemed to have lost the sense of a shared mission, a calling if you will, that had characterized an earlier generation. Perhaps it was a cultural change, an era of me-first where the rallying cries were: "Where's the job?" "Show me the money" "What's in it for me?"

We still carried out our intensive therapy weekends for clients who stutter but it was getting harder and harder to find student volunteers for the treatment teams. I began to find that the highs of therapy were not as high as they had been; the lows were even lower and much more frequent. Some days the "used-to-bes" crowded in so close that I had to flee the clinic.

Yesterday came suddenly for me one morning in a course on stuttering for senior level students. In the midst of an impassioned impromptu sermon about professional ethics and the priority of the clients' needs, a student in the first row raised her hand. "Yes!" I thought to myself. "Someone is concerned about these pivotal clinical issues." Then she opened her mouth.

"Like, will this stuff, you know, be on the exam?" she asked.

After the students left, I put on my coat, walked around the long circular hallway and glanced into each classroom. A relatively better-dressed mature man or woman stood at a lectern talking to a group of younger men and women. The young people had their heads down and they were writing; most of them looked as if they were doing penance. Overwhelmed with existential *angst*, I fled the building and went to see Jim Rapport, former department chairman and my Daddy Bear.

Putting aside the script of *Taming of the Shrew*, a play he was planning to direct for the next theater production, he listened intently to my tale of woe. I was too upset to remember everything he said, but one homely yet insightful metaphor Jim offered started me on the path of adjusting my attitude. Combating student indifference, he said, "is a bit like trying to teach a pig to sing. It's a waste of your time and energy . . . and it annoys the hell out of the pig." Maybe it was time to stop annoying the pigs.

When I talked to Lynn about my growing malaise at the university, she said she knew things had changed and not for the better.

"Why don't you consider retiring?" she asked.

"But what about our finances?" I replied. Since I am totally inept when it comes to managing money and didn't even write a check until recently, Lynn has always been the Minister of Finance in our family. I knew she was knowledgeable and could handle budgets—she directed a growing department for the county—but I was dumbfounded when she laid out the particulars for me to see.

"We're in good shape," she said. "The girls have finished college and are well-launched on their careers." Mary was then a ranger at Olympic National Park and her sister, Lynn, had accepted a position at Glacier National Park for the season. They loved the mountains and were thriving in the west.

"Here's what we have been putting aside every month," the Minister continued, showing me some spread sheets. Rarely had I even looked at the amounts on my paycheck during my thirty years in higher education. Although I knew I had signed *something* years ago to shelter some of my university earnings, I was astounded by the bottom-line sums she showed me.

"With the university buy out annuity, the state pension which starts as soon as you retire, as well as the health care benefits they'll provide, I think you should go for it," she concluded.

"Well . . . ," I temporized.

"You seem to be pole vaulting over mouse droppings lately," Lynn observed wryly, using my own maxim to foster her case, "and I know you're not sleeping well."

"Just a little insomnia—but I'm trying not to lose any sleep over it," I joked.

"Enough already with the M*A*S*H humor!" she exclaimed with a chuckle and then turned serious. "Dr. Emerick . . . " Lynn always calls me Dr. Emerick when she wants to remind me that I am trying to play Superman or when I bring my university lecturing voice home to dinner. "Remember this dictum of yours? 'You cannot heal a wound with a dirty bandage.' "

"Right, but . . . " I started, but Lynn interrupted.

"Look, my job pays pretty well and I really like the challenge of running the County's Commission on Aging," she said. "For the past year or more, I've been watching you struggle with the university role. You've always wanted to be a literary naturalist and follow the music of Thoreau. Maybe now is the time."

It all made sense. But still I temporized: To leave, or not to leave. Hamlet in the speech clinic. Then, remembering the sound advice Dr. Charles Van Riper, pioneer in speech therapy and native of the Upper Peninsula, had always given me, I gave him a call.

Many years before, I had asked him how I could repay the field of speech therapy for the help I had received and he simply said, "Return the deed." Dr. Van was now retired from Western Michigan University and enjoying a second career writing hilarious tales of growing up in the U.P. When I shared my ambivalence about leaving the university, he was silent a long time and then he told me this parable:

> An eighth grade science teacher put a frog in a pot of water and asked the class to watch closely. Placing the container on a burner, he slowly

> turned up the heat. The frog floated happily as the water gradually warmed—it seemed to go into a sleepy torpor. As the temperature increased, the frog continued to nap, never moving, never showing concern. Finally, as the water began to boil, the frog died as the astonished students watched. Removing the dead frog, the teacher then selected a live frog and, ignoring the gasps of his students, plopped it into the boiling pot. The frog immediately jumped out.

"Think about it, my friend," Van said enigmatically and hung up.

That night, Henry David Thoreau came to me in a dream (maybe it was the anchovy pizza), stood at the foot of the bed with a look of wild surmise, and uttered this quote from his book *Walden*:

> "To affect the quality of a day, that is the highest of arts."

And so I whistled as I walked away from the academic life. Some of my colleagues expressed surprise, wondering why I was retiring at the age of 53 and at the top of my career. Former students called or wrote and said that I couldn't leave, that it would make them uneasy to know that I was not holding down my old post. When a student reporter came to interview me for an article in the campus newsletter, *North Wind*, I paraphrased my literary mentor:

> I left the profession of speech therapy for as good a reason as I entered it. Because it seemed to me that I had other lives to lead and could not spare any more time for that one.

Yet, before I could get on with those other lives, there was one more brief Camelot in Arizona which allowed me finally to leave the groves of academe with good feelings.

It was a Raspberry that led to our sojourn at Northern Arizona University. Not a fruit, but a young student, Patty Smith, with the lovely maiden name of Laframboise, which, translated from the French, is "raspberry." When Patty moved from Michigan to Flagstaff, she immediately began petitioning the university to lure me to Arizona as a visiting professor.

Visiting university professors are a bit like celebrities. Students always welcome someone new with enthusiasm; the speech therapy majors at NAU were familiar with my textbooks and clamored to work with me. The temporary professor has no long-term responsibilities and, best of all, attends no meetings. What a deal!

While I taught and supervised therapy three days a week, Lynn was a volunteer ranger in two nearby national monuments. The rest of the time we explored Arizona, enjoyed the hiking and visual wonders, and soaked up as much of the Native American cultures as we could.

I had a number of Navajo students and I came to admire them greatly, particularly for their deep relationship to the land and how they maintained a balance between their traditional way of life and the demands of modern society. One student had translated a standard diagnostic test into the Navajo language and was invited to present her work at a national meeting in Chicago. The evening before she left on her first plane trip, her medicine man conducted a blessing ceremony with corn pollen to ensure her safe passage through the outside world.

The Arizona time was very meaningful as an epilogue to my teaching career, but by the time we returned to our native valley in Upper Michigan, I was eager to commence the next chapter in my life.

The lure of other lives to lead, especially a life revolving around the natural world, was so intense that I could resist no longer. This land, this wondrous region, this beautiful Upper Peninsula had burrowed deep into my soul and I felt compelled to portray its many charms in words and pictures.

Maxim # 9 ***If you can't change the facts, try adjusting your attitude***

Don't waste energy doing battle with conditions you cannot alter. Instead of obsessing upon the barrier, focus on what you can change. Typically, that involves looking at the situation from a different point of view.

As the leader of nature hikes, I am continually amazed at the narrow range of comfort exhibited by some participants. A bit of rain, a few insects, an uneven trail, temperatures deemed too hot or too cold, and a myriad of other conditions elicit complaints. Since I believe we should meet nature on its conditions, I am not very sympathetic to such lamenting.

Fortunately, my ranger daughters taught me how to deal with whining. It's simple: The leader whines first. It works like this let's say the path we are following takes a turn up a hill. The leader, in an exaggerated moaning voice, says, "Ooooh, nooo, you didn't say we were going to go up hill..." Usually, the participants look at each other in bemusement, grin and then keep whatever complaints they may have to themselves. ***Sic transit*** bellyaching!

Beware also of "ancient mariners", those poor woe-be-gone individuals who continually want to tell their sad tales. They seem to relish their misery and love to share their personal albatross with each new unsuspecting listener. They cannot, or more accurately will not, respond to any assistance directed toward remedying the situation. Characteristically, their response to any advice as to how they might improve their lot is the refrain, "Yes, but..." and then a litany of "reasons" why it would not help.

When someone persists in a course of behavior which is unpleasant–even painful–then we must look elsewhere for an explanation: No one stays in a position of discomfort unless some need is being satisfied.

Whenever I need a quick attitude adjustment, I repair to some remote environs and perform the Dance of the Wild Cucumber. Let me vouchsafe to you how to do this dance: bend slightly at the waist and knee, shuffle forward and sing (while holding your thumb to your nose and extending your fingers skyward).

Tweedle de dee
Tweedle de dum
All hail immortal nose and thumb.

KEEP LOOKING FOR THE PONY

We are well into the second event of our annual triathlon and the participants are all having a great time. The entrants are close together in one small pack, holding a spirited discussion about the relative merits of Slovenian and Greek food. An hour ago, we mounted bicycles and made our way from downtown to Marquette's premiere recreation spot, Presque Isle Park. Stashing our bikes near the entrance, we are now walking joyfully around the perimeter trail. We are spirited because we enjoy each other's company and because we know that the third and final event of our triathlon is approaching—feasting on an ice cream cone from the park's snack shop.

One strawberry, three chocolates and a raspberry cone later and after some lively debate about how to age gracefully, we cycle slowly home. Thus ends another monthly gathering of the Thoreau Sauntering Club.

Henry David Thoreau was addicted to sauntering about his native Concord, Massachusetts. He described his sojourns in the forests as idle roaming in search of nature's secrets.

Our sauntering club has no dues, no bylaws, no rules or order. No minutes are kept—although some cynical observers consider that we are wasting hours—and we tolerate no rancor in our ranks. The monthly outings are planned around a quiet ramble in the forest and then, over tea and scones, we hold discussions on a wide variety of topics.

The Sauntering Club was launched several years ago not long after I retired from university teaching. It was not difficult to find a small coterie of recently retired friends also eager for new adventures. Having been physically active all our working lives, we knew better than to retire to the stereotypical rocking chair. Here was an opportunity to really explore this incredible native valley in which we dwell, the Upper Peninsula of Michigan. We would strive (with John Muir) to be *in* our world, not just *on* it. Now that we had the time to saunter and savor the rocky hills, extensive forests and miles of Lake Superior shoreline, we would endeavor to be in harmony with nature. We would nourish our spirits by inspecting frozen waterfalls, and pay our annual respects to spring wildflowers and the autumn color spectacle. Following Emerson's advice, we would endeavor to be in harmony with nature. "In the woods," he wrote, "a man casts off his years, as the snake his slough, and at what period soever in his life, is always a child. In the woods is perpetual youth."

There is nothing like having exuberant ranger daughters stationed at the nation's crown jewels to help a former academic rediscover the natural world. Lynn and I were very proud of our daughters. They were independent, doing important work and living in beautiful places. They wrote well, penning some extraordinary poetry of the natural world and their experiences in it. Best of all, they wanted their parents to come each summer and see, up close and personal, the parks, forests and mountain ranges they loved. They guided us to places that only the rangers knew—remote alpine lakes in Idaho's White Cloud Mountains, Anasazi ruins in Arizona and Utah, little known trails in the North Cascades and High Sierras and a wild and scenic river in the Steens Mountains of Oregon, to name only a few.

Like many identical twins, Lynn and Mary are very close but always disliked comparisons from people trying to identify minute differences between them. They did find amusement in one episode of park ranger confusion. When they worked in the National Parks and wore the standard uniforms, even friends found it difficult to tell them apart at first. Consider the family of tourists who attended a campfire talk given by an attractive dark-haired ranger at the Grand Canyon with the name tag: Emerick. Four days later, the family stopped to pay the entrance fee at Olympic National Park and thought they were seeing the same ranger named Emerick!

When the girls achieved red card status and begin to fight wildland fires each summer, I was naturally apprehensive. Their descriptions of the work were graphic: acrid smoke that blinded eyes and provoked respiratory distress; soot and grime that refused to wash off, even if showers had been available at outpost camps; crowded camps and undistinguished food; long hours with their crews on the fire line wielding heavy tools in oven-hot air. They loved it.

When we could coax them into telling us why they liked firefighting so much, they got a far off look in their eyes, almost identical to the expression I had seen in the eyes of Korean and Viet Nam war veterans when they were able to describe their combat experiences. There was something about being so close to danger, Mary and Lynn said, that made forest firefighting a focused, intense experience. All one's senses and energy were focused on this singular task; they had never before felt so alive. They spoke quietly about the close friendships and camaraderie which grew from these summer fire seasons in the west. They were literally touched by fire in their youth and it changed their lives forever, especially when they lost close friends in the battle.

I'm sure Lynn and Mary have never told their parents about most of the dicey times they have had on the fire line. But we were caught up in the tragedy which took the lives of 14 young firefighters at the South Canyon fire near Glenwood Springs, Colorado in 1994. The morning after the disaster as we waited at home knowing that Mary had been fighting a fire in the vicinity, I received a frightening call from the Forest Service.

"Hello, is this Mr. Emerick?" the caller asked.

"Yes," I said, not daring to take a breath.

"Do you have a daughter named Mary?" the lady asked again.

"Yes . . . yes . . . ," I responded.

"We just wanted you to know that she is safe. She was not injured in the fire. We've asked her to call you," the caller reported.

I was so impacted by simultaneous shock and relief that I am not able to recall any more of that conversation, what I said to the Forest Service representative or any of the other information she may have given to me.

When Mary did call later, she was overcome as she told us that her close friend and one of her house mates for several seasons at Florida's Panther National Wildlife Refuge, Roger, was one of the smoke jumpers who died in the massive blowup on Storm King Mountain. Roger was from the small Upper Peninsula town of L'Anse, fifty miles away. Mary was given a leave to attend the funeral. Watching her and a squad of other young people standing beside Roger's casket in yellow fire shirts, dark pants and heavy boots precipitated an intense flashback to the terror of my own near-death experience in a propane explosion two years earlier. I realized that for Mary and her colleagues, as it had been for me, the sudden realization that at any moment the bottom can drop out of our lives, is life-changing. It alters your sense of security while at the same time you become intensely aware of how fragile and precious is this life we are given.

While searching for an elusive whitetail buck on Halloween eve, I was confronted with a sharp reminder of personal mortality. I had rented an old farmhouse near Bark River in Delta County for some late-season archery hunting. Mike, the farmhouse owner and guide, reported that deer were plentiful and that he had seen a dandy trophy buck on his 200 acres of farm and forest land. Since the weatherman predicted it would dip well below freezing overnight, Mike ignited a propane space heater before he left for his home in town. The furnace seemed to be functioning property when I turned out the lights and went to bed. Little did I know that leaking gas was pooling in the basement while I slept.

About 5:30 a.m., after delaying the inevitable as long as I could, I finally had to roll out of my warm sleeping bag. Muttering something about needing another half-hour of sleep, I decided that I might as well stay up and enjoy a leisurely breakfast before heading out to hunt. Flushing the toilet, I moved to the wash basin and turned on the hot water. The world erupted.

A gigantic explosion rocked the old house, blowing out the windows and plunging the room into darkness. As the room swayed violently, debris rained down on me. Fireballs swirled and snapped like giant phosphorus pinwheels in the inky darkness. I could smell the acrid odor of my hair burning. A second explosion blew out the walls. The 80-year-old farmhouse did not go gentle into that dark night. The din was horrendous as the upper level collapsed in a terrible crackling, screeching funeral dirge. I could detect another disturbing noise, my own voice screaming in terror and bewilderment. Then a huge beam struck me on the back, pinning me in a crouched position in the wreckage. *So, this is how it ends*, I thought. *All my four decades of outdoor adventures come down to this final horrifying instant.*

Then images of my family flashed into my consciousness: *I cannot yield to the pain and ominous weight. I want to see Lynn and my daughters again.* Calling upon legs made strong by decades of competitive running and an upper body powerful from tedious sessions of pumping iron, I straightened up, threw off the heavy beam, and surged forward, scrambling out over the flattened and splintered bathroom wall.

In shock and disbelief, I looked up and saw the sky filled with stars; never had they appeared so close, so comfortingly familiar. Carefully, I assessed my situation. The house was totally demolished; boards and belongings were scattered in all directions; a thin wisp of smoke spiraled up from what had been the living room. I was bent over almost double in pain and clad only in burned and tattered long underwear bottoms. It was cold—only 22 degrees, I found out later—and frost lay thick on the grass. I felt like the sole survivor of an apocalypse. I knew I had to get help, and fast.

Somehow avoiding glass, boards with nails and live electrical wires, I limped out of the yard and toward the nearest neighbor a quarter mile away. "Help!" I yelled again and again as I approached the darkened residence. A chorus of barking erupted from an outbuilding and, irrationally, I considered retreating. Finally a man appeared at the back door and asked warily, "What do you want?"

After all, it was Halloween morning and I must have been an incredibly scary apparition appearing out of the frost and gloom. My torso was covered with burns and cuts; my eyebrows and hair were singed and I was wearing only tattered underwear and a look of wild surmise. But Ken Gagne took me into his warm kitchen, gave me his own shirt and summoned the authorities. Soon Mike's wife appeared, shaken but in control, and took me to the hospital.

The emergency room staff was astonished that I had escaped the explosion and flash fire with limited injuries and that I was reasonably coherent. Although much body hair was burned off, I suffered only minor burns. I did have a myriad of cuts and abrasions from flying debris. More seriously, x-rays revealed five broken ribs, just inches from my spine. To say that I had been lucky is certainly an understatement.

By the time Lynn arrived from our home in Marquette with clothes and her special brand of comfort, the euphoria of survival was fading a bit. Despite the intense discomfort of fractured ribs, however, I felt compelled to return to the site of the farmhouse and see it in the daylight.

The devastation was incredible—only the foundation of the house was left standing. Fire department officials believe that an electric spark from the water pump in the basement ignited the propane gas. The resulting explosions had been monumental. A large refrigerator was blown 30 feet out of the kitchen; a substantial cinder block chimney was reduced to rubble; smaller bits of debris were scattered more than 150 feet in all directions.

As I slowly made a circuit of the ruins, I kept asking myself, "*How could anyone have survived, let alone walked away from this*?" If I had been any place other than the bathroom, I would have been crushed. Without a doubt, Jim and Vic, hunting companions who were otherwise occupied on that weekend, would have been seriously injured or killed in the blast. As I paused at the exact spot where I had made my miraculous escape, something caught my eye. Bending down painfully, I saw, resting precariously on the splintered, flattened bathroom wall, a copy of the Bible. Of all the books blown out of a bookcase in the upstairs bedroom, it was the only one which had come to rest at the point where I made my exit from the collapsing house.

Nothing concentrates your mind quite so well as a near death experience. While I still experience horrific nightmares about the explosion and become uneasy whenever I catch a whiff of propane, I have acquired a sense of urgency in my new life mission.

When I retired from the university, my goal was to spend the last chapter of my life connecting people with nature. I intended to accomplish this through my writing and by sharing my lifelong interest in birds. Meeting Jim Bruce, then a district ranger for the Hiawatha National Forest, at just the right time, was another one of those synchronistic events which I have learned to welcome. James the Bruce, as I came to call the energetic ranger of Scots descent, and I had a fruitful collaboration on some exciting projects.

We inaugurated an annual breeding bird census to gather information regarding the population density of various species. Each June, an army of volunteer bird lovers fans out over the Forest to gather data about the number and variety of birds in various habitats. Now in its 11th year, the census helps Forest Service personnel monitor population trends, determine the effects of land uses and identify species of birds which may be at risk. As valuable as those data are, I was even more pleased that each new volunteer also became an advocate for responsible stewardship of our natural resources.

But we wanted to lure other, more casual, visitors to learn about the more than 100 species of birds which nest in the Hiawatha National Forest.

"Let's do something very different," mused Jim as we surveyed a likely birding spot near Autrain Lake.

"What about an audiovisual interpretive trail?" I asked. "Let's introduce bird identification by featuring their songs."

The Au Train Songbird Trail, the first of its kind in the nation, is now the most popular attraction on the Forest. At nearby grocery stores, visitors check out a kit which includes a tape recorder, pair of binoculars, bird identification guide and a prepared tape cassette. At observation sites along the two-mile trail, colorful plaques with drawings and descriptions of each bird were erected. The visitor stops at each site and plays the recorder while watching and listening for the featured bird. The tape describes the bird and includes examples of its song. Since birds are quite territorial, they will come close to investigate when they hear their own song.

Over and over again I have witnessed the surprise and enjoyment people derive from watching and learning about birds. Sometimes a single sighting, perhaps of a scarlet tanager glowing in the sunlight, is enough to transform a casual observer into a devoted birdwatcher. In order to promote these opportunities, I launched Schools of Birding. For a day, or even an entire weekend, participants immerse themselves in the world of birds. Using a simple mnemonic, the neophytes learn how to systematically observe and sort out identification cues: How *B*ig is the bird, what salient *M*arkings does it have, how does it *A*ct, where does it *L*ive, what *C*olors does it show and what *S*ong does it have? *B*ig *M*ac *A*nd *L*arge *C*hocolate *S*hake. Corny, I know, but people remember it and it works.

The response has been very gratifying—hundreds of neophyte naturalists have been transformed into enthusiastic birders. Best of all, once they are exposed to this new colorful world in their own backyard, they become advocates. When they see an indigo bunting, hear the flute-like call of a hermit thrush or thrill to a flight of sandhill cranes, they want their children, grandchildren and at least the next seven generations to be able to have similar experiences.

So I have come a full circle, back to the literary naturalist yearning to be free of stuttering so long ago. It feels very comfortable to be home at last.

When you open your heart and mind to the infinite possibilities of life, serendipity has a window of opportunity to enter. Synchronicity is only an option when you have sloughed off the logic-tight compartments of linear, rational thought. Not long ago and not really searching during a ride through the summer splendors of our superior peninsula, we found a log home in the country south of Marquette. The Foster Creek Homestead is located in a pastoral area with huge farm fields, gorgeous upland hardwood forests and densely wooded river bottoms. A branch of Foster Creek flows through the western edge of our 80-acre paradise.

In a small open meadow on our back forty acres, I have erected Woodhenge, a pine version of the ancient stone megalith, Stonehenge. It was the fulfillment of a long Celtic dream. Here we hold gatherings to celebrate the seasons and offer our thanks for this wondrous land. I spend time inspecting morning dews and admiring sunsets. And each day I try to emulate the Navajo students I was privileged to know: balancing precariously with one foot in their traditional culture and the other in contemporary society; yet still greeting each dawn with a promise to walk in beauty.

Maxim #10 ***Keep Looking for the Pony***

Once upon a time, a team of psychologists was asked to discern why Ron and Don, 10-year-old twin brothers, were so different. Ron was a dour pessimist while Don was determinedly cheerful and optimistic.

The psychologists isolated the brothers in two large rooms for almost an hour. First, the team looked to see what Ron was doing in his room, a large gymnasium filled with all sorts of new toys. The boy sat glumly beside the shiny playthings.

"Let's play with the ball and bat," suggested the psychologists.

"No, I would just lose," replied the pessimistic Ron.

"Well, here are some roller skates, how about trying them on?"

"No, I would just fall down and hurt myself," countered Ron.

Each time the team offered a new toy to the child, he responded with some glum or worried excuse.

Next, the psychologists entered Don's room, a large stall filled with straw and manure. The child was ecstatic. He was leaping into the air, burrowing into the piles and laughing happily.

Why are you so happy in this room filled with manure?" the psychologists asked. Pausing only a moment, the twin replied, "With all this manure piled around, there just has to be a pony in here somewhere!"

EPILOGUE

The urologist slipped the x-ray into the frame and turned on the light. Without preliminaries, he pointed to a dark shadow and pronounced:

"That's a large tumor in your bladder and, if I were a betting man, I would wager it is cancer."

I pulled my chair closer; his body language said I was invading his personal space. Perhaps he thought I was about to yell, gnash my teeth or weep on his tie in bitter anguish.

"Well," I said finally, "maybe it's a Jimmy Hoffa body part—and we will both be famous."

He turned slowly and gave me a thorough inspection to see if I might need an injection.

"But," the urologist said slowly, emphasizing each word as if speaking to a child suffering from delayed development, "how would it have gotten in there?" How could he have missed the joke?

"Who knows?" I replied. "The Mafia works in strange ways. And you know, it could even be Monica Lewinsky's chewing gum."

A faint grin appeared on the physician's face. However, ignoring my humor—he later told my family doctor that I had seemed nervous—he proceeded to offer, as physicians are inclined to do, the worst possible outcome of impending surgery. At the end of his dire tale, I borrowed a line from desert iconoclast Edward Abbey and said, "If all that does occur, then at least I won't have to floss my teeth any more." Still the humorist after all these years.

One of the stereotypes about older people is that they often parade their medical syndromes past anyone who will linger for the recital of body symptoms. A long time ago, when I was just a young boy and not old enough to take part in the annual deer hunt, my grandfather invited me to be the aide-de-camp. My job was to cut the wood, help the cook of the day and clean up the dishes and pots after every meal. I loved it because I got to be with the men and hear their stories. When hunting season commenced, my grandfather took me aside and admonished me not to ask Bert, one of his hunting cronies, how he was.

"Don't ask him that, Lad," Grandfather warned. "Because he will tell us all about his ailments, from bunions to scalp psoriasis. We don't need a bloody 'organ recital' in deer camp.' "

So, eschewing a lengthy organ recital, the surgery was successful, the chemotherapy was not too bad and at present I am feeling well. After the medical procedures I have been even more productive than ever—leading bird walks, writing at least a dozen articles about nature topics and nurturing the Thoreau Sauntering Club.

One astounding experience reinforced my growing conviction that there are no accidents in our lives.

Not long after the surgery, I was browsing in a local bookstore in search of new reading material. Since my retirement, I focus almost exclusively on topics about the natural world so it was with some interest that I picked up a volume by Sandra Steingraber titled *Living Down Stream.* Good, I thought, I am fascinated by individuals' adventures with regions of the country or natural features such as lakes or rivers. Picking it up, I flipped the book open to page 255 and there in large bold print were the words BLADDER CANCER. So moved was I that I almost swooned. Diane looked up from her computer behind the counter and asked, "Are you all right,

Lon?" I nodded yes, bought the book without saying a word and, still in synchronistic shock, went home to devour its contents.

Dr. Steingraber was using the metaphor of living downstream from toxins which have been released into the air, soil and water by mega-agriculture and manufacturing companies. The most compelling aspect of her book is that, as a cancer survivor herself, as well as a respected scientist, she tells of a personal investigation into the link between toxins and carcinoma. Without our permission, she shows, industries have for decades been conducting longitudinal experiments with our bodies. Is it not possible that toxins in the air and water can, over time, trigger our genes into a deadly metastatic dance? Now, I thought, remembering all the nights so long ago spraying DDT, here is a worthy cause for me to pursue with whatever time I may have left.

This I know for certain: There is no time for "shoulds" in my life. Whenever someone tells me that I "should do this" or "should do that," I offer this litany: First I do the few things that must be done—servicing my truck, shopping for groceries, paying the bills. Secondly, I then spend the bulk of my time doing what I *want* to do—a very long list. And then, if there is any time left—and usually there is not—well, that's devoted to the *shoulds*.

Happily, I have no lingering regrets that I should still be helping the speech disabled. Been there, done a lot of that. I do miss the classroom and, even more, being a mentor and a minister of encouragement to young people. But I continue to adopt "daughters" wherever I happen to fetch up: Janel in the Forest Service; Jeanne, a local speech therapist; Nancy, an aspiring writer; Luann, health care worker and another cancer survivor; Heather, a struggling Ph.D. student.

We met Nancy when we moved to the country a few years ago and came to admire her devotion to home-educating her children and living gently on the land. Learning that I was a writer, Nancy asked hesitantly one day if I would look at some material she had written about her family's life on Big

Creek Farm. I said, "Sure," but sighed inwardly. Many want-to-be writers have asked me to help them with their manuscripts and most of them were so terrible that I found it difficult to comment without dashing the aspirant's dream.

When I sat down to read the two chapters Nancy left with me, I was astounded. Her prose flowed, it sang, it brought tears to my eyes. Her writing was so good it made this author ashamed of himself as a writer, as was Hemingway when he first encountered Beryl Markham's *West with the Night.* It is good to know that there are fine writers, like Nancy, my daughters and others who are picking up the torch and bringing their own fresh experiences in the natural world to the page and to new audiences.

The professor cannot resist leaving with one last bit of advice. An important aspect of a satisfying, whole life is a relationship with nature. I am talking about a serious bonding with the natural features of your local area: identifying the watershed where you live; learning about the rocks and soil; celebrating the seasonal fragrances; learning the trees and flowers. Let the land bury itself deep in your heart.

There is, I think, a deep yearning in humans to touch the land, to feel the pulse of the planet. We remember somewhere deep in our memories that we are, despite our dazzling technological marvels, still creatures of the earth.

Each of us needs a listening point where we can reconnect and feel at one with the natural world. I have found the goal of my own pilgrimage here at the Foster Creek Homestead. I wish for you a special place—in the woods, by the water, in a park—a listening point from which to savor this precious planet.